## MORE PRAISE FOR
### *HIROSHIMA IN THE MORNING*

"If remembering lies at the heart of all memoir, the best memoir goes far deeper, asking questions about the propulsive nature of time, the consequences of forgetting, and the treacherous liberations of solitude. *Hiroshima in the Morning* is a memoir of the most sophisticated kind, a lyric, a quest, a universal poem."
> —Beth Kephart, author of *A Slant of Sun,*
> a National Book Award finalist

"Rahna Reiko Rizzuto's new book is intimate and global, lyrical and clear-eyed, a compelling personal narrative, and an important social document. Here past and present, Hiroshima and 9/11, interweave to tell a story of unendurable loss and tragedy but also of tenacity, survival, and rebirth."
> —Lauren Kessler, author of *Stubborn Twig: Three Generations in the Life of a Japanese American Family*

## PRAISE FOR RAHNA REIKO RIZZUTO'S
### *WHY SHE LEFT US*

"A ferocious first novel. . . . Bold and disciplined. Rizzuto's talent for creating vivid scenes, for getting inside strong emotions, for writing with great power, is unmistakable."
> —*Newsday*

"Rizzuto's characters are wonderfully well drawn—jagged, honest, and unpredictable."
> —*Washington Post Book World*

"An enigmatic and engaging novel. . . . Rizzuto wisely leaves the mystery that drives the story intact, even as she explores it from every possible angle."
> —*Los Angeles Times Book Review*

For if Hiroshima in the morning,

after the bomb has fallen, is like a dream,

one must ask whose dream it is.

—Peter Schwenger

RAHNA REIKO RIZZUTO

# HIROSHIMA

## *in the*

# MORNING

**THE FEMINIST PRESS**
AT THE CITY UNIVERSITY OF NEW YORK
FEMINISTPRESS.ORG

Published in 2010 by the Feminist Press
at the City University of New York
The Graduate Center
365 Fifth Avenue, Suite 5406
New York, NY 10016
feministpress.org

This publication was made possible, in part,
with support from Dr. L. Diane Bernard.

Second printing, March 2011
Cover design by Think Studio, NYC
thinkstudionyc.com
Text design by Drew Stevens

**Library of Congress Cataloging-in-Publication Data**

Rizzuto, Rahna R.
Hiroshima in the morning : a memory / by Rahna Reiko Rizzuto.
   p. cm.
Includes bibliographical references and index.
ISBN 978-1-55861-667-7 (alk. paper)
1. Hiroshima-shi (Japan)—Description and travel. 2. Rizzuto, Rahna R.—Travel—
Japan—Hiroshima-shi. 3. Hiroshima-shi (Japan)—History—Bombardment,
1945. 4. Hiroshima-shi (Japan)—History—Bombardment, 1945—Personal
narratives, Japanese. 5. Atomic bomb victims—Japan—Hiroshima-shi—Biography.
6. Pacifists—Japan—Hiroshima-shi—Biography. 7. Hiroshima-shi (Japan)—
Biography. 8. Rizzuto, Rahna R. 9. Rizzuto, Rahna R.—Family. 10. Japanese
American authors—Biography. I. Title.
   DS897.H5R59 2010
   940.54'2521954—dc22

                                                                  2010019658

*For my children*
*Forever and for everything*

# CONTENTS

# PROLOGUE

# LEAVING

**I** CAN TELL YOU THE STORY but it won't be true.
It won't be the facts as they happened exactly, each day, each footstep, each breath. Time elides, events shift; sometimes we shift them on purpose and forget that we did. Memory is just how we choose to remember.

We choose.

IT BEGINS IN OUR HOUSE, on the top floors of a nineteenth century brownstone. I'm sitting at our long dining room table across from my husband Brian, my two, brightly-pajamaed sons asleep—finally—after slipping downstairs for water, and then just one more kiss between the banisters. The year is 2001, the place New York City, and in the quiet of the last, warming days of May, I am making a list.

I am a list maker, a super-organizer who measures her success in life by how many of the items she's checked off. This is who I've always been, and it's never occurred to me to question it. It occurs to me only that I have a goodbye party to throw for myself, which will involve a twenty-five-pound pork butt, Hawaiian rock salt, and ten yards of purple plumeria-patterned fabric that I've ordered on the internet but has yet to arrive. If I think about plates, about feeding fifty of my dearest friends who will come to wish me well, I will not have to think of this trip of mine—my first trip away, my first trip alone, my six-month long "trip" to the other side of the world.

Brian watches me busy myself. And then the question: "Why are you going to Japan?"

I lift my eyes—the answer so obvious that it hardly seems possible his question is real. It is, in fact, *impossible* to consider his question, to glimpse just the broad shoulders of his doubt before it escapes into the shadows, to hear the bass notes of sadness in his voice. Impossible because these things would trap me.

Even looking around my home would hold me here.

I will come to believe, months from now, that life is a narrative. That who we are, what roles we choose—that these are deliberate characters we create to explain what we did and find a way to face tomorrow. That memory is not history. That we rewrite ourselves with every heartbeat. At this moment, though, my life is still a given. It does not—despite the contradiction of reality—change. My life is what surrounds me; I subsist on it so entirely that I can't begin to see it. The air I breathe is the air that still shimmers in the spot, just above me, where my enormous belly and I once stood on a scaffold, in a bikini top and a pair of baggy sweatpants, spackling the ceiling three weeks before my oldest son was born. I still draw sustenance from the echoes over the kitchen floor where my children love to dance during dinner. Echoes that shrink, cool, fade but do not, even over lifetimes, completely disappear. I am more than anchored to my world; I am tied tight like Gulliver by the tangle of past poses and years—mine, Brian's, my children's—toe here, breast, belly button, wedding ring. In the room, in the trophies from every trip Brian and I have taken since we were teenagers, there are so many flags that say *we were there*, and *there*, and *there*. There are decades of a life that's far more tangible than I am. And it's not just the *there*, the good life, that I am dangerously, paradoxically blind to—it's the lack of my own identity, the utter, unqualified *we*.

Instead, I take inventory: I have stocked the freezer with food, put all the "to do" papers together for my sons' upcoming school year; I have rearranged our babysitter's schedule so Brian will be able to get to work on time and won't have to race home in the evening. He was there when I did these things. When I found the ad for the fellowship, he was the one who urged me to apply. I had rejected the idea: it was too unplanned for, this grant that would not be awarded for a year and then could be postponed for another. It was not absolutely essential. Six months to live in Japan, to do whatever I wanted, when I only needed three weeks, a month at most to do some research for my book. And yet. How else would I get to Hiroshima? The thought kept sneaking back, tangling my feet. There was an urgency growing— inexorable and obscure—even though I had no visual, of

Japan, of absence, of myself, to guide my journey. I was the one who raised the idea in the first place, and though I could not picture myself leaving, still, I filled out the paperwork.

And then I won.

Brian had plenty of help with the children. And, he himself pointed this out, he had always promised to be their primary caretaker, so he owed me a chunk of time. Once the decision was made—the lying on the couch together, the press of flank to flank and Brian's assurances, not even whispered, that everything would be fine, he could handle it, they would come visit, maybe even for half the time—it became oddly easy to forget the fact that I'd never lived on my own, for six days let alone six months. That I had never lived in a foreign country, spoken another language; I'd never set off without a plan tucked carefully in my pocket and an extra copy posted on the fridge. Something about this opportunity had exploded all my patterns of behavior: I, the domestic center—the mother of babies, really, of small boys ages three and five—came to see no portent in leaving my family with four telephone numbers in my backpack and not many more Japanese words in my head. But in my own rush to manage, and his inclination to ignore what's in front of him and hope for the best—"how" had been the only question until this moment.

"Because I got the grant," I replied.

IN BROOKLYN, IN 2001, I was making a list. I knew I was leaving, but if I had known how thoroughly my life would shatter over the next six months, into gains just as astonish-

14

ing as the losses; if I knew I was saying goodbye to the person I was that night, that decade, that lifetime; if I understood I was about to become someone new, too new, someone I was proud of, who I loved, but who was too different to fit here, in this particular, invisible narrative that I was sitting in but couldn't feel, would I still have gotten on the airplane?

This is the question people will ask me. The question that curls, now, in the dark of the night.

How do any of us decide to leave the people we love?

# PART I
# IF HIROSHIMA

*The things that you forget to prepare yourself for:*

*Locking the door.*

*Walking away from the house.*

*—First diary entry, June 19, 2001*

|

## JUNE 19, 2001

|

THESE ARE THE THINGS I packed:

— Twelve blank notebooks (paper is more expensive in Japan, or so I am told);
— Three hundred tablets of Motrin IB and a bottle of 240 of the world's heaviest multivitamins;
— Forty-eight AA batteries in case my tape recorder dies mid-interview once a week, every week, for the six months I'll be away from home;
— Twenty-four copies of my first novel to give as *omiyage*;
— Two never-opened textbooks on how to read kanji.

THESE ARE THE THINGS I KNOW:

Hotel rooms in Tokyo are so small you can't turn over in your bed without knocking your shampoo into the sink.

Identically suited salary men surge forth like lemmings every day for a fifty minute lunch.

Before I land, I should at least know how many islands Japan has, and what they are called.

Five hours down. Seven hours and six months to go.

# TOKYO

I AM WALKING IN SHINJUKU STATION. Me and Ellen and the one million, nine hundred and ninety-nine thousand, nine-hundred and ninety-eight other people who come through this place every day. And as much as I loathe the thought of being a wide-eyed tourist, this is not, and never could be, a train station.

It is Oz.

It is miles of shopping. Kiosks, salons, restaurants, boutiques, pharmacies, grocery stores, bookstores—stores within stores, on top of stores, kitty-corner to other stores. I tick them off, each as marvelous as the one that will come next: I can get a cell phone here; a toy; envelopes for weddings, funerals, and birthdays; perfume; a *happi* coat; wine from France. Anne Klein is underground, right next to agnès b. And for those passengers returning from Kyoto who haven't yet bought a gift for everyone they know, there are sweet, folded *yatsuhashi* in sets from six to forty-eight. They sell art here—actual paintings in the subway. But of course, this is not the "subway." This is wide, bright, incredibly clean. There are no homeless people here, and all the smells are good.

These are my thoughts as Ellen strolls beside me. It's my second day, a day of rain in Tokyo, and I've been brought here because, here, I can gawk all day and never get wet. It's not that the city is strange, not exactly, not in the way of being unimaginable or never before seen, but still, I seem to be having a hard time filtering. In my rush to understand, to label and characterize—in my excitement—I've lost even the basics of perspective because, in the same way I might experience the sun moving across the sky, Tokyo has become a parade. I've walked from the train station itself to Takashimaya, and then through a second department store, over a covered bridge piped with American pop tunes, to a Kinokuniya bookstore with an excellent collection of English-language fiction, all without going outside. Now, back in the general perimeter of the train station, I'm still ticking off the floats: this one is the basement of yet another department store, where Ellen can buy some beef for her stroganoff dinner.

Stroganoff as a gift from the hostess, perhaps. A reminder, for me, of home. It was one of the few dishes my mother used to make, the kind with cream of celery soup in a can, that went along with the green beans and fried onions in a can, the boxed Jell-O, the short list of food from the 1950's. My memories maroon me: the green beans especially, and the three-tiered gelatin mold that was featured at every Thanksgiving with my mother's side of the family, the one with the cream cheese layer that no one ever ate.

There are few occasions to think of such things anymore. I'm still unused to the silence that ushers in the subject of my mother, or the irony that she resides more and more in my memory even though she is still alive.

Every time Ellen asks about my parents, I add a few more trifles to my standard response. By now, I am used to evasion, perhaps even good at it. Since my mother's illness became apparent, I haven't had the occasion to spend so much time with someone who knows her, a friend who could pick me out instantly at the customs gate in the airport—me, the differently shaded replica of my mother—and who would hug this stranger to her as a long-lost child. Ellen will give up five full days of her life for me, to take me every single place I need to go, want to see, or might like to experience if only I knew it existed. She merely smiles when, on my first day in her small suburban neighborhood, we must stop three times on the way to the train station to take pictures of narrow two-block-long side streets because there are signs outside the shops with kanji on them; we snap picture after picture of one or the other of us standing in front of shrines smaller than a bedroom, which must be captured on film to send back to New York for my children since they have never seen these curving, organic roof lines tucked under like a turtle shell, tipped up like the wings of a bird. Roofs with snakes' scales, edged in armor, fish dancing on their bones, cranes sleeping on the mossy, wooden ribs that fan out above them. These animals whirl in my head—who knows why one is here and not the other?—and if I don't capture them now, there may never be another chance. Ellen indulges me without once mentioning how ridiculously small my vision is. It's her pleasure to care for the poor foreign child who doesn't speak Japanese . . . But I am not a child. I'm a thirty-seven-year-old mother who should be equipped; who should have left my home once in a while; who should not still need a mother—and even though I say I don't, and Ellen says of course I don't, it's still more than nice to put off that moment when I must determine which ". . . *mutter mutter gozaimasu*" means this is where I'm supposed to get off the train. If it was a bit of a shock that, after three months of language study, I was finding it impossible to guess where individual words begin and end in both written and spoken Japanese, it was at least a perfectly acceptable reason to be coddled . . . until Ellen assured me that she doesn't speak Japanese either.

In Tokyo, I am beginning to realize, you don't *need* to speak a word of Japanese.

The young woman at the J-phone shop wearing blue contact lenses speaks English. The hawkers on the streets in front of the nightclubs do, too—and many of them are do-rag adorned, Fubu-wearing African American men whose very existence suggests that genuine hip-hop style will rub off on all who enter there. Every building and storefront in Roppongi has English on it: WELCOME, BIG SALE, LUNCH SPECIAL, HEAD STORE, STARBUCKS. Every restaurant has an English menu you don't even have to ask for. Of course, Ellen can buy beef in a department store basement. She can spend fifty dollars on one hundred grams of meticulously marbled meat, she can spend twelve dollars on a peach. Beneath the layers of the latest New York and Paris fashions, she can peruse a kaleidoscope of sustenance, from jellyfish to pancake mix, all without a word of Japanese.

It isn't the gift of borrowed translation, then, that I'm relaxing into. It's the possibility that life here might be possible. And if I am not aware of it yet, if to be aware of it would mean admitting my fear—which is precisely what all my intense and dogged efforts to ignore the fact that I was going to Japan were designed to obscure—still, I can feel a loosening. As I watch Ellen select her groceries with no task more unusual than placing her bread on a plastic tray in the bakery section; as Ellen smiles at the cashier and takes the bags she needs to pack up her own items after she pays, all without actually speaking to the girl behind the conveyor belt who seems to be effusively thanking us for visiting the store, I can allow myself to acknowledge my journey. I am here, in Japan, and it *is* an odd, crazy place; it *is* halfway around the world, the farthest point on the globe from my real life, but there's no reason to be nervous. I don't have to learn anything to get along here, about them or about myself. I don't have to change or find myself lacking— Japan has accommodated me, and long before my arrival.

This is going to be easy—that's what I think. Walking next to Ellen, on our way to make some stroganoff, I can clearly envision how simple the next six months are going to be.

|

# AUNT MOLLY'S VISION

|

AUNT MOLLY SAW THE CITY when it was not. She told me about it the first time we met, but I wasn't listening. And my deafness then—almost eight years ago now—is the reason I've come to Japan.

Molly arrived in Hiroshima in 1946. Too late to see the lily of the valley lamps that hung in telescoping arches over the Hondori shopping arcade, or the men in creased black suits and bowler hats, or the ladies they escorted. Ladies who trailed hems of flowers around their covert ankles, who were replaced by workers scurrying in *monpe* pants; men who were never replaced but simply disappeared. Too late for the bomb, for the sea of fire, the endless bed of concrete stones. My great-aunt was one of the few Americans who ever saw the burned-out city, but by the time she got to Hiroshima, people were already building shelters on the small plots of the wasteland where their homes had stood. Where their brothers and sisters had been incinerated. Where they'd returned to gather their mothers' gleaming bones.

In those days, if you hiked even a short distance up the mountains that ring the Ota River delta, you could still get a clear view through the ghost of what once was Hiroshima, miles away to the shore of the Inland Sea. But there was already a black market where people sold what they had, and bought what they could, and ate dog meat without caring what it was. There were soldiers (albeit Australian and

English because the Americans were being housed in radiation-free zones) giving chocolate to begging orphans with the stock benevolence we have all come to recognize from the movies. Hiroshima was manageable by then—if not a city, then still a place. If not alive, then at least no longer dying.

Or maybe she wasn't too late. Molly's children still remember joining the peace marches in Berkeley while they were in strollers, or at least old enough to cling to them, or to cling to the high hand of their angry and determined mother as the people on the sidewalks screamed "Commie go home." They remember the antinuke meetings, the visit from the Hiroshima "maidens"—young, crippled, disfigured women who were sponsored by the Quakers to endure months of surgery to reduce their scars and repair the damage. They remember playing in the other room to avoid seeing rare footage of the wreckage that one of the antinukes got their hands on: even glimpsing it through a doorway would give Molly's daughter nightmares for years. When I first went to California to interview my mother's aunt, more than fifty years after the bombing, Molly was full of Hiroshima, haunted and desperate to get it out. She wanted to break the silence.

But I didn't want to hear.

This is what haunts me now: How could I have come into adulthood in America without knowing about the atomic bombings? Once I was faced with a family member who'd actually been there, how could I have chosen to ignore? Perhaps I was afraid of the tremble that came into Molly's voice when she talked about it, or of exposing my own ignorance. I found it much easier to stick to the topic I'd come to discuss: the internment camps, where Molly and the rest of my mother's family had been banished during World War II. That was a wartime embarrassment I was familiar with— the makeshift barracks in the desert where the US put its own ethnically Japanese citizens—an episode I had control over by having already spent a year exploring its limits and parameters. My first novel was inspired by my mother's discovery that she herself had been interned as a child, and my fantasies about what secrets and safeties such a silence might contain. Aunt Molly may, at that point, have been one of the few people still alive who had lived the unique Japanese American triptych of the internment, the American occupation of Japan and the atomic bomb aftermath, but I didn't know that. The interview with her was one of the last I was doing to wrap up a book that had already taken shape. That was the truth: I had come with one topic, and couldn't allow my aunt to stray too far from it. The bomb was too risky to conceive of. It was too big a world.

But then, when so much time had passed that I could no longer vouch for a single detail of my meeting with Aunt Molly, I started having nightmares of my own. I was walking through an atomic wasteland. Fires burning, buildings at my feet. I had lost something; I was searching—I was walking on ashes through a place where I'd lived, that should have been familiar, but which would never again hold the things I loved, or even resemble the world I once knew.

I didn't know what I was looking for in my nightmares,

only that I never found it. I woke with a fist in my chest, and an awareness that, of course this had something to do with Hiroshima, but also with my mother. I was embarrassed at knowing nothing, at ignoring my mother's recollections of a time when she herself had been in Aunt Molly's living room avoiding the "crazy peace people" with her cousins, so this was my mother's history too, however glancing, that I had lost.

A memory, then, from that interview: my great-aunt, single girl in her twenties, in a shiny black car with the doctors. They are going house to house; they are visiting the mothers of stillborn babies. Molly is a file clerk for the Americans, or a statistician, but she can also be an interpreter. She can ask the grieving mothers for the details—where were you when the bomb dropped?

She can ask for the body of the dead baby.

I remember her every word, "I thought we were helping."

When she found out—and how did that happen?—that she was the enemy, that the US government was classifying all that information so no one could fully understand what the bomb did, that they were offering no help and no medical care—and here begins the outrage—that's when she became a peace activist.

I am almost sure that's what Molly told me. I had no other source of information, so it had to come from her.

But when I returned—just over a year ago, surrounded by silence, suffocating—to really listen to her story . . .

Molly had finally forgotten.

"That trip to Japan was the highlight of my life. I'm not sure why I decided to go. I wanted to see it, and on some level I knew I was doing something unique that had some historical value. But any young person going out and traveling, even if there isn't a war, is going to be changed.

"You see how other people are living, and how they look at things differently. They have different concepts. I was changed in that way. But the biggest thing was, I realized that I was not Japanese. That no matter what I went through in America, being evacuated—that was terrible—I was shocked that the Japanese Americans were being put into those camps because I really believed what I had learned in civics class, that if you were an American citizen, you were born with certain rights. I mean, I really believed that, and the next thing I knew, I was behind barbed wire. And it made me question—I mean there I was, a teenager, singled out and put in a camp—it made me question whether I was a real American.

"But when I got to Japan . . . there was no way I was Japanese either. If I just walked down the street, kids would run after me and say: 'A-me-li-can, A-me-li-can.'

"And here I was, with a Japanese face. But they knew."

—Aunt Molly

# I

## HIROSHIMA

I

I HAVE BEEN WAITING FOR HIROSHIMA. I have never seen
a photograph, yet I will know it exactly. The rocks there
will sing to me, the grass will smell like home. Or maybe
the sea will smell like home. There is a legitimate question
of what home smells like, whether it's the ocean I grew up
fishing in in Hawaii, or the smell of cooked rice, or a flower,
or a spice that I've never bothered to catalogue because, how
do you record such a thing, like a heartbeat or a breath? I
have become a New York mother, but I was a Hawaiian
child, and though it surprises me, it is still my earlier home
that comes back to me on this island nation: in the com-
monalities of ginger and nori, and the edge of déjà vu. It is
only now, when that child reincarnates so clearly, that I first
encounter the possibility that that self was ever gone.

Why am I here? And why do I keep asking myself why
I am here? I have always scorned and disbelieved anything
that can't be articulated, and yet I must know that "*to collect data, to research . . . "* cannot account for the joy I feel,
and the terror. I need this journey, and that vague awareness
leaves me in the unfamiliar territory of instinct. If there *is*
more than meets the eye, I can relax, and yet, I must be sure.
I glance out the window as I blast through tunnels. Each
time I pull my ears out of the darkness and pop them, the
world is a little greener, the roofs more pitched, more tiled.
But each glance is also more of the same, more of the subtle

move out of the flatlands and away from the boxy grey cities that have flanked so much of my journey—subtle as so much of Japan has been so far, which is to say, so familiar and so different that I have no ability to judge. It is maddening: I cannot distinguish between what to keep and what to discard.

Could I be so ill-equipped, and after so many years of successful living? Or have I refused to equip myself, preferring to stand weaponless in my new world? I have moved from ignoring to blithely refuting. If you sat beside me then, I would tell you—in the same voice that I would use to regale you with the transformation of New York's subway—that I am not used to trains. That there aren't any in the US, or at least, that our distances lend themselves to cars and airplanes, nothing like this sleek *shinkansen*, with its red, roving bubbles on the LED sign in the front of the car that inform me I am now traveling at more than 330 kilometers per hour. Perhaps it's the jet lag, or my growing sense of being unmoored, but I am suddenly back in the time, more than fifteen years ago when I was just out of college, when Brian and I went from Madrid to Barcelona on a crippled, backwoods cousin of this train, through an endless countryside of farms and hills lit up with the small quick flames of cypress trees. That was the last train I rode in; the last time I found myself moving, bodily, between places I'd yet to imagine. We had been heading for Italy until the standby travel company that had already taken our money gave us the choice between Madrid or another night in the airport, so I was loose, on my first trip to a foreign country, in much the way I have been let loose now. Then, I had Brian beside me; the boy who grew up in Europe, who loved to please, to give. And what he gave was my first glimpse of a new world, my twenty-year-old hand in his, surrounded by his knowledge, navigated by him. If it seems too plump, too bright in my memory, that is what memory is—the youth and young love, the excitement of exploring, Jack and Jill, each amazing new sight a gift from him to me. I leapt then because he was leaping with me: going to Spain "because." I can still taste the capers in my mouth, huge, grape-sized pockets of salt and puckering. I can still hear the old man who grew them asking if Brian and I had sex. I pretended not to understand the language, but the question made it clear: we were already married, from the moment we met. From age seventeen, we were together every minute that could be wrenched away from school or work.

WHEN THE TRAIN PULLS THROUGH the last ring of mountains, Hiroshima is suddenly new. In its buildings, in their height and orderly placement, newer than most of the cities I've seen so far. Of course it makes sense—the whole place was crushed by the atomic bomb in 1945 and then burned to the ground by the intense heat, so of course there are no ancient pagodas, no historically winding streets—but it is not what I expected. Not the home I was sure I'd see. It strikes me then, with the force of the first time, that I've entered a foreign world. Not foreign as in Japanese, but as in the fact that I can't imagine what tomorrow will look like, let alone what I will do on that day. On this train, without a fearless leader, I am experiencing a new sensation. A laxity, a sense of not being quite attached, head to spine to fingers; a sense of being too small to claim the vast space in my seat, or to walk the aisles of the *shinkansen* without tumbling over my toddling feet. If I had to put words to this new feeling, I would have to say it seems to approach the definition of "lost," at least a little. Or maybe it's the feeling of being lost that's approaching me—there on the train, a seated target— maybe it is loss, not surprise, that ripples through my tongue every time a bite from my *ekiben* turns out to be salty instead of sweet, fishy instead of vegetable-based.

Perhaps loss has been with me all along.

I survived Tokyo. Saw sights, got my very first cell phone, met the people who managed my fellowship, and smiled the "making conversation with strangers at a wedding" smile. And now, when by rights I should be savoring this moment of time apart, of time alone, which has never truly existed in my life, instead, I am thinking of Ellen. As the train begins to wind down its journey, I understand that Ellen's image is the last thing I recognized, my parents' friend who accompanied me all the way to my seat on the *shinkansen* and then—having tucked my packages overhead and settled my lunch—stood with goodbye tears in her eyes until the warning signs flashed that the train would be leaving, until she could no longer resist the urge to tuck my hair behind my ears and hug me close. If I can no longer assume my way through Japan without articulation, then I must now *do* something to move forward, and I don't know what, or how. I take out my contact numbers—the only link I have with tomorrow—and run my fingers across them as if to straighten out the digits. I have two organizations listed, and two women: Jane Osada, the Japanese American ex-boss of a friend of my mother-in-law who has invited me to lunch tomorrow, once I am settled; and Kimiko Uchida. But Kimiko, who I haven't even met yet, is already mad at me.

## RUDE AWAKENING

MY MOTHER-IN-LAW IS STANDING on the platform when my train pulls into Hiroshima station. At least, the woman in the middle of three, the one in charge of pointing and peering through the windows, looks just like my husband's mother. The same salt and pepper bob, same broad mouth, high cheekbones. She is clearly equally exacting since the trio is waiting, not just where my car will pull up, but within two rows of my seat. This somewhat stern-looking ghost from my present has to be Kimiko Uchida.

I am no one Kimiko knows. Christopher, who administers the grant, had put me in touch with a friend from his somewhat distant past: a professor, close to eighty, the kind of gentleman who responded to my gift of a copy of my novel with a letter in perfect English, full of praise and apologies for his inability to understand the nuances of the

34

prose. He lived in Hiroshima, and though he did not experience the atomic bombing, he knew a few people who did—Japanese Americans, more to the point; people who speak English. But just before I left New York, the professor was diagnosed with stomach cancer and hospitalized.

Enter Kimiko, his former student and the founder of a volunteer organization that promotes "peace activities" especially for foreigners. I'd written to her at his suggestion, and she told me to get in contact with her when I arrived—conspicuously without the elaborate niceties he included in his letters. But a week or so before I was scheduled to leave, my usually silent phone rang in the middle of the night with the news, from Kimiko, that the professor was ill, followed by a slew of questions: Which hotel should she reserve for me? When, exactly, was I arriving? What was my budget? And my other requirements?

We battled the cell phone crackle, the long distance time delay, her humility, and the way her sentences trailed off into phrases like "and so" and "like that" before they could include the essential details of her thought. I thanked her profusely and told her please not to bother herself on my account, the hotel reservation was so much more than I could have hoped for. I would be sure to get in touch with her when I got to Tokyo. And then, while Kimiko continued to make plans for a greeting party at the train station, as she made lists of who would be doing what to help me—all unbeknownst to me—she stumbled onto a tiny piece of information I'd neglected to mention. Namely, that I had also contacted Jane Osada, and she was planning to help me too.

I'd thought Kimiko's offer was simply a required formality so I politely declined because I didn't want to be trouble. But what I would come to learn was, she had an obligation to help me—not just a request from a former teacher, but quite possibly a deathbed request—and she had absolutely no choice but to put everything else aside and complete many tasks to make my life easier. To her, my "please don't trouble yourself" was not a refusal at all, it was simply a way to say *thank you so much for all the help that I know you will work like a dog to give me anyway*. And by not mentioning I knew Jane, by creating a situation where there was even the slightest possibility of someone else duplicating the strenuous efforts I didn't know she was making on my behalf, well, I was just plain rude.

And my apologies, when all this came to my attention, still have not been accepted.

I can tell this by the tone in which Kimiko says it's not a problem. I can feel it in the NASCAR pace we're using to drag my luggage from the train platform to her car. When we can't seem to find a working elevator to get me and my American-sized possessions to the parking lot, I am sure of it. I am one of those bad gaijin—the kind who, when someone doesn't seem to understand her request, just repeats it louder, shouting if necessary, in English because these people around her must all be deaf.

At least I know better than to try to justify myself. I apologize. Keep apologizing. And whenever there's a lull in the conversation, I apologize once more.

"SO, WHERE ARE YOU GOING TO LIVE?" Kimiko asks me. This is the third time around for this question. A foreigner in Japan needs to have a sponsor in order to rent an apartment. Kimiko's candidate for sponsorship is the Japanese government, since it sponsors the overall grant, or perhaps the grant administrators. She is not pleased to hear that, once here, I am entirely on my own.

The repetition then, as I struggle to learn this cultural lesson: Is she asking me to suddenly remember I have a sponsor in my address book? Or to agree to stay in a hotel for six months? Or to take this problem to someone else?

We are having miniature cups of coffee in the lobby of the hotel she reserved for me. Me, Kimiko, and the other two women, who have been introduced to me as "choir members." Apparently, the professor is a singer among his many other talents, and these women are connected to him through song. They are speaking to me in Japanese. This surprises me; it's the first time anyone has tried to converse with me in Japanese. I am trying to follow and I imagine Kimiko is annoyed that I don't understand *anything*, which might be why the English translations, when they come, seem to contain about four words for every forty. The two choir members are smiling and nodding as they choreograph a stationary dance of self-congratulation for having successfully completed their mission, which was to hand over the names and telephone numbers of three of the professor's Japanese American friends who I might want to interview. I appreciate their help, but I'm feeling just a little needy, and the simple fact that the greeting party seems somewhat

37

outsized for the small bit of information I've been given makes me hopeful that there's something more to come. But as the coffee cups empty, it doesn't seem so, and on the truly important points—like where am I going to live for six months and could it really be possible I might not be able to find an apartment?—they fall silent.

They take stock. I have a cell phone, some yen in my pocket, and an adequate budget. The hotel reservation Kimiko made is for a week, so there's a place for my enormous bag at least until our biceps recover. The interview contacts have been duly passed on, so unless there's something else I need . . .

With this last good deed ticked off, with the gentle, closing snap of their notebooks, they palm the scalpel to cut the only cord I have and assume that now I can breathe and eat on my own. Probably, I can. Maybe I'll be ready to try it tomorrow. But it seems I am not ready yet.

"Would you like to have dinner?"

Kimiko's perfect lipstick is perfectly still, only her eyes move as she appraises me like a crocodile submerged in a river. I am sure she's wondering why in the hell I can't just live in a furnished hotel room for the next six months. My invitation to dinner is accepted, but it will have to wait until after eight, because she is very busy. Oh, and to get things straight, since I'll be here longer than any other foreigner she has ever had to babysit . . .

Tonight and for always, dinner will be dutch.

IF I COULD ONLY GET MY MESSAGES, everything would be fine.

If the "simple menu" on my cell phone had not simplified out the English instructions for how to retrieve my voice mail, perhaps I would be coping, not reduced to tears in a faded *yukata* in a chilly hotel room with the rain outside my window. If I was still in Tokyo, I could have walked up to any bleached blonde, Starbucks-drinking Japanese person I passed on the street; any school girl in pigtails and uniform and extremely loose and baggy athletic socks that look like leg warmers, that drag on the ground and have to be held on the leg by special glue; pick one, any one, even one in black lipstick, white vampire makeup, or platform shoes that are taller than her head, and that person could surely have shown the poor foreigner with her first cell phone—how is it possible that a New Yorker in the twenty-first century has never even held one in her hand before?—how to access that little icon.

But in Hiroshima, in the streets and even in the J-phone shop, no one speaks English. Not the first sales clerk, who I literally drove into the back room with my question. Not the second, who was pushed out to face me after much giggling in the back, along the lines of—I understood this much— "You go out there, no you!"

AND MAYBE, IF I HADN'T GONE to the school to meet Jane today, if I had taken the J-phone encounter as an omen and turned around on the wide, straight streets, retraced the perpendicular intersections, and walked through the other pedestrians who all look neat and conservative and purposeful and completely oblivious to me and back to my concrete hotel, I would still be myself. It was just that she seemed so familiar, so much like my grandmother, down to the rolled curls in her hair and the eyeglasses bouncing on her chest from a chain. We had a nice meal, and then coffee, and she promised to help me get some business cards, and gave me a few names of people who I might interview. And then, as I was leaving, she put her hand on my shoulder and said that I should call her anytime, because it can get a little lonely, and I found myself in tears. It was that space again, the space from the train opening up; the reminder that I have always had someone to ask, someone who would help; that I have never been lonely in my life. And though I kept telling myself that I'm not lonely now, I am excited, I can do this, my eyes seemed, just at that gesture, to disagree. I'm not like this, I wanted to assure her, I don't cry. But I couldn't form the words.

OR IF I HADN'T DECIDED to write her a damned thank you note, maybe this wouldn't have happened. Maybe if I had a real place to live and didn't have to spend fifteen minutes digging through a suitcase, strewing wrinkled possessions around the room because I can't find my stationery, and if I can't find my stationery, I might as well never leave my hotel because I simply cannot survive in this world of never-ending gratitude without it. I can't organize myself. I can't find the quiet to write, or a place . . . I can't even get access to my email. I want my keyboard. I want my printer. I don't know what I'm looking for anymore; there is something I need but it's not in the bag. It is not among the things. I want this to be easier, even as some part of me understands that it's not so hard.

I want my life.

BUT FINALLY, TRUTHFULLY, maybe if I hadn't called home. Not in this mood—though if I can't talk to Brian when I'm frustrated, when can I call him? And who else can I call? There is no one—then maybe I wouldn't be hearing his voice, the voice of a man I spent my entire adult life with, and finding myself unable to speak. In his voice, I can feel the embrace of the life I had, a sweetness, a fat that fills the rooms that he walks in, that would wrap itself around me if I walked in them too. I want to tell him that there are good moments here, that I have learned to drink cold coffee from a can out of a vending machine and that tomorrow the sky will be blue. I want to share that with him, and also to show myself that, although I may be inexperienced and not as prepared as I'd hoped, I am strong enough to meet these challenges, and those moments should not feel so thin. I have lived alone for a week: it is done, complete, no longer potential. Why does it feel so paltry in the grand scheme of all he has at home?

I am trying to make my tears as soundless as possible,

though of course he can hear them. And I know he is also crying, and even though I have been away from home for eight impossible, ridiculous days, he asks, in a voice that cracks, "What are we doing?"

That's when I realize that we are doing something. Not watching or waiting or marking time to the end, but taking action. My tears are not simply a bit of homesickness, they are for loss. We are in the process of change. I don't know why we're doing it, or what it is, and I dread it as fiercely as I want it.

But the fact is: it is already done.

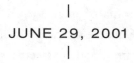

JUNE 29, 2001

ON MY BOOKSHELF, there is a photograph of a fat, naked infant. In his mouth, his mother's nipple. On his arm: a long black burn. His belly is white and creamy. His head is bald and scarred; it is the surface of the moon, pulling on his mother. Dark, pocked, thirsty.

Turn the page and see a girl in a white blouse lying on tatami. Stained tatami, on her back. Her hair is intact, and one unharmed hand that waves in the air, afraid to land. She is alive, for the moment, but her face has been burned away. Her nose and lips flattened into feathery, white ash. The oval between her collar and her hair: white, grey, black, charcoal, dust. This girl lives on the bookshelf; she is alive in my mind. Her faceless image resides in me, her head without eyes. And the irony does not escape me that she was left, before the final darkness, with the flash of the atomic bomb—a vision, some say, of great beauty—and I am left with hers. I am looking for her in the Peace Museum, life-sized as she should surely be; I'm like a child digging at a wound to relish the pain, to extend it, feel it travel down my arm, into my elbow, until it rings in my ears. I want to face her. I want her to save me.

She is not here.

## | PEACE MUSEUM |

FOLLOW THE MAP TO THE PEACE MUSEUM. Cross the bridge, past the heat shimmers, stay on the concrete. Where the Otagawa splits and becomes two rivers, there is a peace park. It's the slim finger of land that lies almost directly under the bomb's hypocenter, the spot that Hiroshima now calls "ground zero." It was once a town called Nakajima, a thriving neighborhood that served as a hub for shipping and open air markets; now, it's a subtle oasis of more than seventy monuments, statutes, and broken stones, with names like "the merciful consoling Kannon for the mobilized A-bomb victim students." Look for the Peace Museum at the base of the park: it's the grey block building on the grey stone plaza; it sits perpendicular to the grey slab walkway extending to, and through, the elegant, arching stone cenotaph that contains a register with the names of all the confirmed victims of the A-bomb—seventy-seven volumes in size. If you stand in the center of the plaza, on the other side of the Peace Museum, you can line up the cenotaph so that it frames the A-bomb Dome. The dome is one of the only ruins left in Hiroshima, a great, spiked skeleton of the Czech-designed Industrial Hall, which escaped total destruction only because the blast was almost directly overhead so there was no horizontal force to blow it over. Once the very image of European grandeur, its broken brick walls now stagger as if the builder suddenly lost his train of thought.

The Museum begins with the crawl of air conditioning on sweat, a fifty-yen admission ticket, and a commercial against nuclear weapons. I slip around that easily; the voiceover is unctuous, and the sentiment—one small step for man, one giant leap for peace or something along those lines—is not what I came for. If it doesn't start with a bang, still I am confused by the deluge of excuses for the bombing: the walls are lined with images of Hiroshima as a military city; of its residents celebrating the occupation of Nanking. The displays in the first room, on the first floor, assure me that the US only decided to develop the bomb because they thought the Nazis were trying to do so. Two freestanding slabs are papered in letters protesting the nuclear tests by governments around the world, each signed by Hiroshima's succession of mayors. There are nearly six hundred letters, almost identical, as if, one leader to another, there was nothing new to say.

*Hiroshima has made a protest to your government against nuclear testing as many as twelve times only in terms of the last year . . .*

*Such an action is absolutely not permissible . . .*

*We vehemently protest . . .*

*. . . a rash act, ignoring the wishes for survival of the human race . . .*

*Hiroshima has made a protest.*

In the center of the room, there is a cityscape: an aerial view of Hiroshima after the explosion. It's a barren circle with rivers, a couple of shattered walls, and a handful of sticks scattered near the edges. You could call it a model, except that that word implies a third dimension. When the bomb exploded over Shima Hospital, every building within a one-kilometer radius, except for three or four made of reinforced concrete, was completely demolished. I know this; why can't I feel it? I have read about the firestorms that ripped through thirteen square kilometers and turned everything to ash, but they are not here. People and animals were vaporized, carbonized, melted, crushed, poisoned, maimed, and burned. Everyone within one thousand meters of the hypocenter was dead by the end of the day if not immediately. Almost everyone within two thousand meters died within weeks. I have seen these pictures, read the tallies. All I know of this city, this country, this journey I am taking comes from the books that say those who drank water died. Those who ate fruit may have had more of a chance than the others. Those who weren't even in the city, but were hit by the black rain, or worked in the rescue effort, also died. Total casualties over time: some two hundred thousand people.

And now, I am standing in the resurrection of the model, in a cold, quiet building shaded in grey. On the second floor, in the next hall, the next rooms, I am awash in the dedicated revival of the city. This is Hiroshima's "life must go on." There is all sorts of hope here, and good will, and I know this is the "Peace" Museum, but isn't that a euphemism? Isn't this a museum of war? It is not only that I have yet to encounter any of the images that brought me here; I cannot see the point to building a paean to forgiveness. Forgiveness is forgetting, erasure, absence; it's all the blanks in my family's history, the expediency of accepting what isn't real. The Peace Museum is the one place, if there is one place, that could hold America's feet to the fire and say: *look what you did here*.

Where is the bomb?

MY MOTHER'S FACE sways in and out of darkness as she and I move through the museum, eyes checking in with each other as another door shuts behind us, before the new one slides open. A different museum, a distant time. We are the only visitors in the Museum of Tolerance, the only two being moved from room to room through life-sized, too-real sets of the Holocaust, an audio narrative telling us what is happening now—to the Jews we are today, during this enforced, hour-long tour, this programmed exhibit from which there is no way to turn back.

46

We have been given name cards, each with an alter ego, a Holocaust survivor or victim, though we won't find out which until the doors to the last room have closed.

It is 1999, I am in Los Angeles to promote my first book and my mother has joined me, gaily and repeatedly chattering about flying from Honolulu to meet me "in the middle." It's unusual for my mother to travel alone, odd that she would want to sleep in the same hotel bed. At the time, I thought it was just her excitement about my novel, which she'd come to see as her own, based on her life story, though it wasn't. Now, one museum to another, remembering my mother's face hovering in the dark replica of the gas chambers, I wonder if she had a different impulse that she left unspoken—if she could feel menace in the words that were already spilling out of her head, the thoughts she couldn't access, even the small acts she had performed then lost track of—and she'd been trying to create new memories, just in case. In hindsight, my mother seemed anxious, and we both were cold in the rooms that turned inevitably into stone walls and death. When we were finally released into the light of Los Angeles to plug our name cards into the waiting machines, we found neither one of us had been spared.

Now, I cannot shake the vision of the card in my mother's hand, or, rather, the hand itself, how veined it was, and thin. I cannot shake the shame that the memory I created, even inadvertently since neither of us knew anything about the Museum of Tolerance except that it was walking distance from the hotel, was one of shepherding my mother unsuccessfully past death. My mother died in the Museum

47

of Tolerance, and if I did too, if everyone will, it is still a punch in the gut. My mother died. Is dying.

It is a question of time, and time is the question. How does one spend it? When does the part about living your life to the fullest begin to shift into just making do, and then into suffering, and how do any of us know where we are in this process? When I first found out about my mother's illness, I wanted to leave my life and go home to sit vigil with her. I didn't. She said she was fine, didn't want to have to "entertain" visitors; she wanted to hear the news of the world, the news of my growing young family. She let me imagine I was pleasing her by taking active, almost frantic care of my children, instead of avoiding the pain, the boredom, the anger, that came with waiting for death.

Of course, death is not on the current docket. Death is a melodrama. It is erosion we are dealing with. Already, my mother is not who she was. I can measure that by my father's words, "Sometimes she makes more sense than I do," which come more frequently, and ring more hollow. They safeguard all her flashes of wit and wisdom.

But with every passing day, there is less of her.


THE HIROSHIMA PEACE MUSEUM is almost empty in the heat of this weekday. It is as if history itself has become a tomb best forgotten. I know this can't be true, that busloads of schoolchildren and tourists must visit all the time, and that today they just happen to be touring pop art instead. As I walk down a long corridor, a bridge, to the west building, the silence around me heightens my feeling of dislocation and niggles at my growing belief that this whole Japan trip was a bad idea. Brian is unexpectedly moody. I have been in Hiroshima almost a week, and the fact that I've been unable to report progress—no discoveries, no interviews, not even a home yet—has him at a loss. What have I traded this time for, these twelve days we did not spend together in New York? Though I know I'm not being lazy, that I am trying everything I can to get started, what Brian has refrained from saying is also true: I didn't plan well. There was a time when I thought six months was too long, that I could wrap up my research in three weeks, a month tops. What happened to that efficient person? It's a question neither one of us is ready to ask.

The light, when I reach the west building, is dimmer. This exhibit starts with a flickering tableau framed in scorched, red brick arches. Several wax figures—a man, woman, and child, or is it two children? Surely it's a woman because she hasn't quite lost all her hair—drip red skin off their hands, pick their way through crumbling walls, against a backdrop of fire, arms extended like sleepwalkers. Here are the pored-over, larger-than-life-sized photos of the survivors resting on Miyuki Bridge, more than a mile and three hours from the explosion. Out of focus, or is it just that their hair has been tufted by the blast, turned into soft black cotton or stolen completely along with pieces of clothing, along with skin and other soft body parts that melted in the heat? There is horror here, finally, but it's a thin scream only. A section of wall with shards of glass embedded in it, warped iron shutters from the clothing depot that stood more than 2,600 meters away. There are tattered uniforms of schoolchildren, each arrayed on its own palate. Twisted eyeglasses. A belt, a bag, a lunch box filled with carbon.

Bits of nail. Bits of skin.

WHAT IS IT I WANT to feel? There's a connection I am missing: a howl. There are people around me now, crying; they're turning away from the unbearable, and all I feel is anger. I know what they do not: Hiroshima has been erased. Whatever the museum shows or cannot show, I myself erased it. I refused the bomb; I would not acknowledge it even when someone tried to tell me. I can't expunge the vision of myself, nodding away Aunt Molly's tears, smoothing the family history so it could be put away. This is my shame now: I was impatient for the tidbits of internment and impervious to the discussion of wholescale slaughter. At that point in my research, I was merely following a map I knew, savoring the confirmation of right turns, of alleys and the angle of light in the corners where certainty bloomed.

Now I don't want to forget. Without memory, what is left? Only the present, which, as I've come to realize, may be less "real" than the past. If my mother is no longer who she once was, then when *was* she? When was the last time she was herself, at her best? And if I can't say, exactly, if I can't locate a specific person in the timeline and say "this is it; this is her essence," then how do I comprehend my mother now? How do I comprehend Hiroshima?

The world is forgetting what happened here. The museum, for all its remembrances, is forgetting what happened. Is this what peace is, this forgetting? I cannot accept this. Over and over, I have proven myself to be part of an amnesiac society—in my excuses, my inability to feel, my plain old refusal to acknowledge the existence of something that was right in front of me, I erased the *hibakusha* just as surely as the bomb did, and I cannot accept that this is what peace is supposed to be. I erased the girl without a face, and now I need to know: Who was she? What did she look like? I came to the Peace Museum to be confronted by this girl and hundreds of thousands like her, to be their witness, at last to see:

*The pattern of a crane, burnt into skin.*
*The shadow of a woman, etched into stone.*
*A hand without fingers. A mouth without lips.*
*The space where there was once a nose.*

I came for resurrection. But all I found is the space inside me, and around me, opening, in the absence of certainty.

"There will always be people who seek you out. They like to talk to foreigners, practice their English. They will help you, and they are good to know. But look for the other people, even if it takes some effort. They are the ones who are worth finding."

—Christopher Blasdel, grant administrator

# JUNE 30, 2001

"*Moshi, moshi* . . . uh, Professor Katayanagi-san wa . . . "

Is it "wa" or "ga" I am looking for, and how do you say "gave me your name"? The ridiculous part is, I know this person speaks English, but somehow I've gotten it into my head that it would be more polite to begin in Japanese.

That is, if I knew Japanese.

"Would you like to speak in English?"

That's her, not me. I introduce myself, and my project, and tell her the professor gave me her name because I'm looking for Nisei like her, Japanese Americans who would be willing to tell me what it was like to be "the enemy" in wartime Japan.

"Ah," she says. "Isn't it hot?"

It turns out that she is busy. Very busy. She has lots of family visiting in the summer. They are not coming soon, in fact they have just left, but still somehow, she slides away from me. I can't get a direct answer—yes or no; she won't give me anything to push against or respond to. I ask her to suggest a date when it might be more convenient for me to call, and she tells me about her grandchildren. I ask her to suggest a more suitable month and she wonders aloud why so many Japanese American children don't know Japanese. She's beyond slippery, she is completely ungraspable. Then, when I finally accept that she has rejected me completely, she tells me where she lives and offers, "But come by for tea any time you're in the neighborhood." And I don't know what that means.

*"Moshi, moshi . . . "*

It's variations on the theme two more times. By the third call, I give up the notion of speaking Japanese, but English doesn't seem to help my cause. I speak to a gentleman who is ill and doesn't feel like he can help me. I speak to a woman who's not well either, and who also feels that it is perhaps too hot at the moment to have a conversation. She is not an exceptional person, she doesn't really have an interesting story, and would surely waste my time. But all I have is time. I try to channel the flow of the woman's response, to assure her she can help me immensely, that I can see her any time of any day of any month in any place she finds convenient. I can arrange a meeting well in advance; I can do it on ten minutes notice; it will be air conditioned; I will feed her . : . I am grasping, groveling. I want a yes, but any answer, even a no, would be better than this sliding maybe.

She invites me to call her back in a month.

# FAITH

IF I MADE A LIST of the things I am, the word "capable" would appear on each line. I am the writer and also the scientist. I don't free write; I don't waste time. I have faith in this self who would never strike out in a direction without knowing where she wants to end up. Why then, in Japan, can I get nothing done?

I am browsing books in the stacks of the library because I can't find anyone to agree to an interview. No one seems to understand my Japanese, which is to say that my Japanese is not understandable. I've become a writer who cannot read, cannot decipher the signs—those conveniently posted train schedules, the menus, the headlines. I am a writer who cannot write: I cannot copy down the word for something I want to show to a clerk. I am not fluent in the dual life of kanji characters; I am not fluent even in the usual hour for lunch. I have called the two organizations I had contact information for and am still waiting for a live voice to answer the phone at the World Friendship Center. While I wait, I've spent three days in a row sprawled on the vinyl floor between the sliding stacks in the Peace Museum library, writing things down. I'm collecting facts I never could have found in New York, facts I will surely need. I'm filling pages, plugging coin after coin into copy machines—surely this could be called progress? Why then, do they feel dead to me? They're dragging me down, distorting my story until another day is over and I pick up my boorish American body and my illicit sports drink and go back to my hotel with a single book and a single question: how can I begin to imagine with all these facts in my head?

I am tired. *I am done*, that's what I think to myself, though I still haven't done an interview let alone found a place to live. The law of the land that insists all foreigners must have a local sponsor to rent an apartment seems to be incontrovertible. People from countries that do not wield chopsticks apparently cannot be trusted to put wet garbage into paper bags or take their empty shampoo bottles with them when they leave. Kimiko has said she might be able to arrange this later, "when you are ready." Instead, she suggests I should meet her friend, the director of the Peace Museum, but again this is vague, and since I've been spending most of my days in the Museum library, a required hello to the man who runs it is not on the top of my priority list. What I need is housing, a place large enough for my family when they arrive, but every time I ask, Kimiko exhibits mild surprise that the question is still floating between us. It's clear that I've become a bully, the answer is no, and yet, since there's no one else who can help me, no other way to get a yes, I can't let it go. I have lost faith in myself, am beginning to dread the way each conversation with Brian opens: "Did you find a place to live?" Every *no* an agitation. It raises the question of why I am here, and why I should remain if I'm so incapable of something I could have done in New York with one phone call.

I REMEMBER THAT PHONE CALL, the one when I was still in college. I was moving out of the dorm after my junior year and into an apartment with Brian. It was my father's reaction I dreaded—his role was to object, on upright, moral grounds, and my mother's was to make peace and deflect tension. So it was a surprise when my mother was the one to fret about how young I was, much too young to live with a boy, and even more of a surprise when my father shut her up by pointing out that Brian could change the light bulbs, and *take care of things*. What things those might be, and why he thought I couldn't take care of them myself, didn't occur to me. I was delighted to have gotten away with it—that's how it felt, like sneaking out, rather than growing up. It was not the adulthood I had dreamed of because in no way did I think of myself as adult.

It is unusual for me to be thinking so much of my mother. There's been no time during her illness to dredge up memories, and no room in the life of one family to dwell on what might be happening across the ocean. Now the past is coming unbidden. Little hauntings, memories rising and even twisting themselves, elongating into what I might have wished had happened, rather than what actually did. The conversation with my mother now seems longer than it must have been. Once we got beyond my announcement that I was moving in with my boyfriend, it turned to consultations, at least in my memory, about the relative merits of futons and pillows over more structural furniture. My mother would have liked that—the small details, feeling that she'd contributed to some important decision; she would have liked hearing I was safe, being assured by humor and the petering out of every topic of even remote importance. It is still my habit to be funny in the long emails I write home from an internet café near my hotel, regaling Brian and my father and my friends with my abortive attempts at lunch and the girls at the J-phone shop. I get few responses, possibly the effect of having to painstakingly type in all the addresses each time and the fact that AOL keeps bouncing my mail back, but I do it for myself; it's my way of feeling not so alone. It takes a while to get into the mindset of the intrepid traveler, a woman who would never mention her nostalgia for those things she once was equipped for, her new dread of the scope of sheer opportunity, and the exhaustion of always having to be prepared. Brian never comments on my travelogue, nor do my children, so I write for the image of my father at his computer, waiting. In my mind, he prints out my notes and carries them into the TV room where my mother spends most of her time now, and I can hear my mother's laughter at the funny stories from Japan that my father reads out loud—I write, in that way, for my mother.

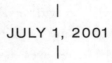

JULY 1, 2001

LUNCH IS:

Ramen from 7-Eleven.

Two *daifuku*—soft mochi balls filled with red bean paste, which no self-respecting Japanese person would eat more than one of—and an Asian pear.

Something from the bread shop that looks like a sausage twisted in bread dough.

*Yakitori* sticks from 7-Eleven.

Chocolate bars from 7-Eleven.

In New York, we don't even have a 7-Eleven. Do we? I don't think I've ever seen one before.

TODAY, I FORGOT that the Japanese generally eat lunch only between 12:05 and 12:55 p.m., and that most restaurants close by around two. At three-ish, I realized I hadn't yet had anything but coffee. There is—according to the guide books—a building with two entire floors of stalls devoted to *okonomiyaki*—a local delicacy, a sort of crepe omelet with different fillings cooked on a stainless steel fast food frying surface which also doubles as a serving platter (meaning you pull your chair up and eat off it). I decided to check it out— to eat out alone for the first time since I got to Japan.

The building is in the center of the shopping district, just south of the arcade, but it looks like any office tower. The lighted directory outside appeared to be advertising restaurants, so I went up the stairs. On the second floor, there was a maze of counters, capital I or L or U shaped, hugging small, open preparation areas, partially obscured by the noren hanging curtains printed with the names of each of the businesses. Every stand had been closed and clean for so long I couldn't even smell the evidence of lunch gone by. I kept going, to the third floor, gaining both confidence and nervousness from the sheer lack of people. Here, a few of the stands were still open. Older women, their skin dry from cooking, their hair wrapped in cloth, made me stop in the entrance of the hall, just by being there. I could see that their stalls were menuless and mostly devoid of other customers to deflect attention, customers who could have shown me by their actions what I was supposed to do. I realized that, although I know the words for beef, chicken, fish, and vegetables, somehow I was thoroughly unprepared to sit down and try to order a dish I'd never actually eaten, especially since, at this place, it seemed that the diners cooked their own food. I stood there for perhaps a minute, entertaining the sudden fear that I would accidentally order chicken skin and jellyfish and then have to eat it while the owner stood a foot away. Picture me: weighing the thought of crunching on cartilage against the awkwardness of simply standing in the doorway. As the seconds went by, that became a reason to go.

In the end, I went to 7-Eleven. At least it wasn't McDonalds—where the windows are plastered with pictures of a bun that appears to be filled solely with mayonnaise and three small cocktail shrimp. More on that in the next installment of the gaijin in Japan!

# HELPLESS

THERE'S A LITTLE GIRL in my head with Shirley Temple curls and freckles playing in a dust-swept road. She is the enemy. She looks about six, even though she shouldn't be: my mother was not five when she was released from the internment camp, but no pictures survive from that time so age six is the youngest image I have of my mother, the only image I have from "wartime" was taken after the end of the war. Of course, this little girl—skirt flying, dancing with tumbleweeds—is not my mother, not exactly. She is my first character from my first book.

My mother could not remember the camps, so I invented them for her. That's how my first novel began. I made them up, pulling from a mixed bag of the photographs that could be taken, from the questions that the man with the year-book at the internment camp "reunion" had asked, the man who wandered through the community center full of former internees eating home lunches of sushi rice and teriyaki, searching for anyone in the room who was three when he was three in camp, who might have been in a nearby block, who might have been his friend.

I pulled from dreams.

I created the children first—this little boy, the little girl who was his friend—and even while I was doing interviews, gathering the details of how the brick floors in the barracks had to be shellacked to keep the dirt from rising, I must have known I wasn't dreaming up a "book about the internment." *Write a potboiler,* a kindly, grandfatherly man had told me in passing, in the halls of one of the elder homes I visited to do my interviews. *That's what people want to read. The facts are boring.* His advice stuck, though I was never aware of following it. I began to fictionalize, to trace family ties that could never have existed but could still be realized and, more than that, could be made so persuasive

61

that my mother could fill in her past with them, tucking her adopted life into bed each night without acknowledging its true parentage until it was hers by nurture. I recreated my mother's memories before she began to lose her own, and now she too cannot remember what is real. I have been left with fragments of my own creation, with fictions, and now that I am in Japan, I'm discovering new creations and new memories of my mother—older, different—of times with her that I never experienced.

Like my mother as America's sweetheart.

Like my mother standing beside me, gazing at the A-bomb Dome. More a presence than a physical form, since I know she isn't truly there, but still real enough in my mind and the edge of my sight: a ruffle of my nerve endings as I find myself being pointed toward a thin white crane, stepping out from behind a crumbling wall to pose on one foot before disappearing again in the field of rubble.

WRITING IS UNCHARTED TERRITORY. It is a dream state, stop and start; it is a tangle of words and emotions that may not yield a single page at the end of a day. People ask me: *What is your book about? What do you want to know?* and I always answer, even though I know the answers will change. My first novel was not, in the end, written just because my mother was too young to remember the internment; it was not, as I would often say, merely about family secrets and splintered lives. When I stopped trying to verify the facts and started using them to open my imagination, my story began to circle in on motherhood, and on all the terrible things a mother and child can do to each other. And in that very unconscious preoccupation, which I would have put a halt to had I become aware of it, the novel was about me.

For as long as I can remember, I never wanted to be a mother. From age twelve, when I was babysitting the neighbors' children for seventy-five cents an hour and spent the entire day locked out of the house while they ran wild inside it, motherhood was not for me. I was incapable of nurturing anyone younger than I was: I had a mental block—and a real antipathy—against making hats out of paper bags and other projects children supposedly liked to do. I had a recurring nightmare too: of a child who woke in the night wanting peanut butter, screaming for it when it wasn't in the cupboards, at a time when the stores were closed, when it was impossible to procure; screaming until the only question was whether it would be me or the child who went out the window. Children were greedy by nature; they would not ever, even when I was exhausted, consider my needs. And if this abstraction was based on nightmare and not experience, it felt quite real. As real as the fact that I was also greedy. I wanted my own time, my own money. My own life.

In order to test the possibilities of my own motherhood, I dreamed my way through a novel. I challenged my characters: Were they human? Loveable? Was it possible for them to heal? Under the protection of historical fiction, I explored the bonds and the effects of abandonment—someone else's choices, someone else's pain—until I had written my way out of my nightmares of peanut butter and into the still unconscious hope that love would not require me to be anything other than what I was.

It was only days after I finished that manuscript that I became—accidentally—pregnant with my first child. Yet I still would not be aware of the link between them until it was pointed out to me by a stranger, several months after the novel was published. Even now, such a drastic, unconscious change makes me uneasy. If writing is truth-testing, a way for me to test the worst and see if I can bear it, then what am I testing now? I can feel myself moving again through my unconscious—it's these odd dreams of my mother, for one; she is appearing quite often, even when I'm awake. If my first novel took me into motherhood, where will this one take me? My mother is part of the vehicle, but not the answer yet.

"Many writers write to find out who they are, and what they think, and where they fit into the world. That's what I am doing, but I am doing it by tracing the Japanese Americans. Because, even though I am one, I grew up having no idea about them—as a group, or even as members of my family.

"I have grown up in peace and privilege, with no notion of war.

"So, when you ask me what I am doing here in Hiroshima, I can say I am following the Japanese Americans. I am looking at history through their eyes. World War II, in particular, was very significant for Japanese Americans because they were caught in the middle, and distrusted by both countries. Being "outside" a country, though, also gave them a more objective look at the war. They didn't have a government to spin out rhetoric and tell them what to think, to terrify them with visions of an enemy nation of fanatics and strange food. I am seeking the memories of a select few who were interned in the American camps and then repatriated to Japan to help me weave some very important missing experiences back into the fabric of our history—for Americans and for Japanese people:

"Namely, what war looks like. What it smells like. What tiny bits of humanity are destroyed in each person, daily, in its great tide."

—author's presentation at the YMCA, Hiroshima

# I
## FIRST TESTIMONY
# I

THERE IS SOMETHING MUFFLED in the Japan I've encountered so far. As the goal of my own apartment remains out
of reach, I have moved out of my hotel and into the World
Friendship Center, a halfway house for peace pilgrims looking for a quick dip into Japan and its bomb history, with
western bathrooms and breakfast. The rooms are clean,
and if the location is not the most convenient in the city—
ensconced on a tiny street behind the love hotels that line the
river—the biggest drawback is the five day limit for staying there, after which point, there is another five day option
across the river. After that, I am out of luck. I can stay in a
hotel for the duration or do what the other stray foreigners
in Hiroshima do: leave.

Do I want to give up, or am I just tired of not knowing,
and of not being able to say?

On this, my first morning at the World Friendship
Center, I will hear a noise in the part of the building I was
told was the kitchen and come downstairs to find a young
woman. In this moment, my life will change. I will meet
Ami, a girl who looks much younger than I am, though she
will turn out to be almost thirty, a volunteer who turns only
partially to greet me, her hands busy on the counter with
breakfast. I am too new in Japan to notice how casual Ami's
clothes are: a pair of jeans and a frilly, capped-sleeve white
top; too unschooled in Japanese beauty to notice that her

hair has been combed into a plain ponytail. There are no lines penciled on this female face, no makeup at all; only a mole on one fresh cheek.

"*Ohayo gozaimasu*," I offer.

"Good morning," Ami says, and there it is: excellent English. For an instant, I allow myself to hope that this might mean true communication, until Ami begins apologizing for the absence of the American couple who run the otherwise empty center, who would surely have canceled their yearly vacation if only they could have divined that I would appear. It's a speech as convoluted, as Japanese, as any I've heard so far, but her demeanor—when do I begin to sense it?—is not quite so deferential. Her back is to me as she assures me they will not fail me again, as they did in the stretch when the phone was not answered. Ami herself will do her best to take care of me, she is focused on her task, which is, of course, my breakfast.

I *do* want egg salad for breakfast?

*Like, fried eggs on salad?* I imagine saying this, with some hope, though the chopped boiled eggs are arrayed before me, their vaguely green yokes crumbling, along with the mayonnaise and raw onions I have never been able to stomach and can't imagine eating in the morning.

Ami has turned to place a cup of green tea on the linoleum card table. She smiles. "It's my favorite. All Americans like it very much."

Where, oh where is the vending machine with cold coffee in a can when I need it and why did I ever leave the hotel? I want to refuse, but can't think of what to say as

Ami tosses the salad together and arranges it on lettuce on two plates. Instead, I drink my tea and answer Ami's casual questions about what I've seen so far. Although her way of speaking does seem Japanese, as I have come to understand that term—overly polite, elliptical—her manner is direct, even amused as she notes my lack of progress with the egg salad. She devours her own and then asks, "So, you came here to speak to the *hibakusha*?"

"Yes." This is what I've been telling her for ten minutes.

"And you still haven't spoken to a single one?"

Ami's eyes are warmer than the question and something of a shock. I understand at that moment that no Japanese person has looked directly into my eyes since I got here. As I rerun the calls I've made, and the fact that no one has agreed to talk to me, Ami pulls my untouched plate towards her and begins to eat.

"There are a lot of them, still, though of course they are dying," Ami says. The point of this statement is unclear, though it sounds vaguely like an offer. "You're in luck today, unless you have plans this afternoon? Yamada-san is coming."

Yamada-san, Ami says, is on the board of directors of the World Friendship Center. At one o'clock he will give his testimony about his atomic bomb experience "for the foreign visitors."

It will be my first interview, if you can call it that. It's almost surreal how simple it is, and also how vague. I will hear a real survivor tell his story, and even though I stumbled onto it, still, it is progress. I want to ask Ami about the

68

others, the "lots of them" she mentioned, but I can't figure out how to do it without seeming greedy and inept. Ami's question, *You haven't spoken to a single one?* still stings; it's something I would have expected of Brian perhaps, with its latent American sarcasm, but not from a Japanese woman who must surely understand how I cannot push. I find myself indicating that I will be hard at work on my laptop in my room between breakfast and the testimony, though I can't for a moment imagine sitting alone in my room waiting, and Ami assures me that she too is very busy this morning and will see me at one.

Once Ami leaves, I step out into the streets of this new area of town, making a careful note of my turns so I can find my way back through the tiny houses that all look the same. The sun is beating down on the pavement—Hiroshima is a shockingly concrete and asphalt experience and the *mushi atsui* air calls forth more sweat than a sauna. I am looking for coffee and a doughnut, neither of which I will find, trying to hasten the morning. The center of the city, which I've already explored, is too far by foot and on the other side of the river—even though I know I still have hours to waste, my heightened pulse assures me I could never make it there and back before the *hibakusha* arrives. I can hear how that sounds, "the *hibakusha*," but what else to call him? I have no image of him; he is not mine to imagine. I drift down the street, past the love hotels, distinguished by the fact that their garage entrances are fringed like car washes so no one can read the license plates inside, waiting for the moment when I can turn back to the World Friendship Center. My breath is catching in my chest, just as it does whenever I'm at the top of a roller coaster. It must be excitement, then, though I hate roller coasters. I follow the river, which is low and resembles the runoff from a well-used mop, trying to breathe.

My walk turns out to be longer than I thought it could be in that neighborhood, and when I return, Ami is there as well, arranging individually wrapped cookies on a plate. She greets me without commenting on my absence and waves in the direction of the living room, where people are beginning to assemble. I gather myself, thankful for the notebook I thought to bring outside with me, hovering near Ami until there are several old Japanese women on the sofas, and a family of long-legged Australian teenagers in hot pants and tank tops, and a bag of shrimp chips. It takes me forever to cross the hallway, the living room growing larger with every step, but when Ami seems to have assembled every-thing there is to serve, I reach the threshold.

In the part of the room I couldn't see, there are two chairs, and in them, already waiting, are a female transla-tor and an older man with only one ear. That side of his head is facing me, facing the door so anyone entering can see it clearly. They are dressed formally, in somber suits in the heat.

I find myself moving slowly on the edges, not to startle. I am the last one to arrive. I find a space on the floor and sit quickly, pen ready, in silent protest to the idle chatter around me that had led me to imagine, from the hallway, that the guest of honor had not yet arrived. Surely these people can understand this is not entertainment? The man in the chair does not acknowledge us. I give him my attention, to show respect; to assure him that I understand how important his story is. I try to find a way to look at his face but not the side of his head where the skin has run like wax and there's only a pinhole where the ear canal is.

He begins, without preamble, at the moment the bomb was dropped. He was a third year schoolboy, conscripted by the military as most students were. He was one of many young people who were making pistols for zero fighters, and that morning, that split second before, they were receiving instructions for the day's work, even though by that time, there were no materials to actually make the guns.

He says it felt like being thrown into a furnace.

He talks, or, rather, he recites the events of the day and the weeks and months that followed. His voice alternates with the interpreter's, both absolutely without expression; the story spins out, or rather it races past us, even with the pauses for interpretation, it does not linger. The dictation I am taking contains gruesome outcomes visited on groups: scorched, carbonized bodies mounding the river banks. A list appears, of deaths: his classmates, his teachers, his mother, his aunt. He was expected to die too, this fourteen-year-old boy. This he states. A simple fact.

"We were numb," he says. He is numb now, this man whose face has melted on one side. He was one of a handful of children who survived and he has lived the last fifty-six years without an ear. How can he sit there without crying? How can he relive this experience in front of a bunch of gaijin munching shrimp chips?

What must it be like to carry the bomb on your body? It defines him. But of course, it defines them all.

The story is finished, but more than that, it is complete. He wraps up with some brief comments about the need for nuclear disarmament and then falls into silence. No one seems to hear this last bit. A few hands are raised, a few questions asked. Something is missing—this testimony had all of force of the books I've been reading, which is to say that it's too easy to set it down, but at the same time, he was faithful to his story. What had he said? *It was like seeing through a camera, a different dimension.* This is how it still feels.

The man leaves quickly when the questions have dwindled. Ami sees the visitors out, and joins me in the living room.

"It's terrible, isn't it?" Ami asks.

I don't know how to respond. I want to ask if there's more, if it's always like this. If it is, I've come here for nothing. I am replaying the audience's questions, noting that they were never addressed to him, but to the translator about "him"—as though he was an object. Was it him, then, or the circumstances? Ami's expression, which I'd earlier thought to be familiar in its transparency, is now unreadable, and I don't know how to ask her without seeming rude.

My notes, in my own hand, are enigmatic. "Yes."

Ami has been watching me struggle with her question, and now she smiles. "Yes," she says. "I know lots of *hibakusha*. You are in luck."

|

## SELFISH

|

IAN TELLS ME: "Seven times! I vomited seven times!"

Dylan breaks in—both my boys are on the telephone because this, finally, is a story, a massive event that Dylan participated in by vomiting only three times but he adores his older brother and expects him to lead so he is reveling in Ian's greater bounty, ratcheting up his awe of his brother— and I laugh, grateful to be an audience member instead of the midnight mop brigade. They're creating family lore that will be proudly declared and laughed at for years to come; a memory being rehearsed in my ears:

*"Do you remember the night when I threw up seven times in the hallway? And then Daddy said: 'Ian, are you going to vomit again?' And I said: 'No' and then I turned and went 'blaaaaahh' all over the floor?"*

Brian gets on the phone to confirm, to add the loads of laundry, the hours of no sleep, the final count of beds affected into the boys' report of the evening. He wants to know whether pillows can be washed or if he should throw them out, and he adds this number in too, with a calculation for their replacement. He is tired—that is part of his message—but he's also proud to have taken the family through the fire.

Brian misses me. Not as another set of hands in the bathtub or forty-five minutes more of sleep; his mother is there on an extended visit to help out during my absence, there to swap naps as they all try to recover. He misses my calm, the simple peace that comes from knowing that there's someone in the world who knows your needs better than you do, and that person is there to meet them before you have to ask. And although he doesn't say it so directly, there's a quality to his delivery, to the lovingly detailed minutia, that assumes I would *want* to participate, even in a night of endless regurgitation. That I would want to know it all, to have him relive it with me, so I can take up my pose inside our family frame.

Home is farther away, after only two weeks. There's no danger I'm forgetting my life there, in fact I remember it so clearly I could tell Brian the exact number of amoxicillin bottles I've poured down the throat of one child or the other in my years of young motherhood. Which one cried, which one I had to sit over, lying him on the ground and pinning his arms with my knees so I could hold his mouth open and get the medicine in. The memory of one son catching the medicine in his mouth and spitting it back into my face is my first thought when Brian adds the latest ear infection to his list of domestic upheaval, but to remind him of it now seems churlish. I can't figure out why it should seem so.

I listen, and murmur comfort about the ear infection. I murmur comfort about his mother's lengthy visit and some problem I dismiss with the people who live downstairs. I am waiting for the last three days of their life in New York to be thoroughly covered, for my turn to speak, because I finally have some progress to report. I've done an interview, with another one lined up. I tell him how odd it was—perhaps the effect of translation—how the answers felt packaged, pre-prepared. I tell him about Ami, who has agreed to help me with the translations and how we've been talking about how to get the real story.

I can hear myself, hear that I am rushing to fill a silence, that I'm reporting, not having a conversation, and that Brian hasn't spoken. As I wait for his reaction, I find myself talking—I don't even know about what. I push on, trying not to hear the empty space between us. I want him to know that the trip is not a failure; *I* am not a failure. He doesn't have to know I did nothing to set the interview up.

"That's great," Brian says. "No apartment?"

The boys have to start their day, he tells me—it's Saturday morning and time to get going. And it's late for me, too; time to go to sleep. I dumped too much on Brian just now. I don't know why my mind wandered so far toward my own preoccupations.

"I miss you," I say, stopping myself from adding, "Really." It's my imagination that he isn't listening, or his lack of sleep. "Tell the boys I miss them too."

"We ate the remnants of dried beans. They used to crush the beans to make oil, and take the meat for food, then they'd take the skin off, crush it together and somehow make it into a round cake. That's what they were feeding the horses, but they kept some for human consumption, and I remember that was rationed too. We ate those. We would break it into little pieces and put it in water and try to make some kind of soup.

"Pretty soon, there wasn't even rice, not even brown rice. I remember eating any kind of leaf from any kind of vegetable, and eating ordinary grass. When we ran out of vegetables, everything was eaten. Anything edible.

"Here's another kind of thing we had to eat. *Inago*, the small grasshopper. They said it had a lot of protein, nourishment, so we used to capture them in the rice fields. We'd dry it, cook it with shoyu or something just to get the flavor."

—Seventy-one-year-old male survivor

|

# THREE WOMEN

|

I MUST BE MORE productive now. I have heard the stories of two survivors; I have notes and tapes and no clear idea of what they mean to me. If I had a plot rather than a vague urgency, rather than a need to know, as in *Americans don't know!*, I might be feeling more accomplished. What was it that they did not know exactly; what was this need of mine, which I could taste but not identify? I've been asked, by Ami, by Kimiko, by everyone I've met in Japan: What's your novel about? What do you want to know?

I want to know what war is. What happens? Not who fights, or who dies, or how does the amputated family rise from the ashes, but: What is the subtle effect of fear, uncertainty, aggression, starvation? How do the things we can see and name, even when we think we've survived them, change the people who we are?

Aunt Molly was an enemy in America. She was a misfit in Japan. *Am-e-li-can* they sang to her, but it was more than that, more than children in the street flinging stones at her ankles. She was outside their suffering. Outside her own.

And there were others: women whose names I came across, Japanese Americans who found themselves in Japan for one reason or another during the war. One of them was a "girl monitor," drafted by the Japanese government to translate Allied messages intercepted in the Pacific. Another was a young mother who was sent back during the war on an

77

exchange ship, pulled from the internment camps, reaching Hiroshima just before the bomb. I found them in the books I read in the days before my second visit to Aunty Molly, written by a professor at a University in Tokyo. "Were we the enemy?" the title asked, and now I realize this is my central question. My new book is also about identity and survival.

I have my answers ready now, or rather my questions: What does a person do in the face of rejection? Discarded by two countries, abandoned by family, what behavior is justified to save yourself? And, most importantly, when you are being torn in two directions, how do you decide who you are and where you belong? Kimiko is going to call the director of the Peace Museum and she wants to know what to tell him about my research. But when I try to communicate this new understanding of my novel to her, it seems too odd.

"These women," she says. "What are their names? There might be a record of them in the museum archives."

After a brief search, I have them. "Well, my aunt, of course. And here are two others: Yuko Okazaki and Irene Saeki."

"Who are these women again, what did they do?"

I go over the few details I have, pairing stories with each name.

"All right, then. I will speak to him about these people and we will see."

|

# MAGIC

|

Anything and everything can happen now—can materialize spontaneously any time the telephone rings in Japan.

Today I have a new home; a grand place by Hiroshima standards with plastic floors in the living area, and two six-mat tatami rooms with sliding glass doors onto a balcony that looks out over the Otagawa, one of Hiroshima's six rivers. The river is lined with cherry trees—it's fairly wide and muddy green and tidal. At certain times of the day, children can play sand baseball in the river bed. I can see the city center from my balcony, and, once I get a bicycle, which Kimiko has promised to lend me, it will be no more than a ten-minute ride to wherever I want to go.

Kimiko found it for me; it is right across the river from her house. She filled it with furniture and bedding, dishes and a desk all loaned by people I don't know, people I will never meet. In addition to a full set of necessary furniture, I've been given a microwave oven that doubles as a toaster, an electric wok for making shabu-shabu, three toothbrushes, six bars of soap, and five medium-sized plastic bowls and buckets, all of which are for washing myself before I take a bath. And now, she is whirling in the center of the floor making magic: transformed from stern to child-like, from elegant dress to multi-patterned moving clothes, from "perhaps, we will see" to "get out of the way so they can bring it through the door." *It* being a washing machine, a refrigerator, an air-conditioner.

Kimiko has given me a place for my family when they arrive, a new home. Everything that has walked though her door is a gift to her—for who am I? She has tested her place in the fabric and found thick layers of friendship, and many people who are delighted to return her favors. I'm not the first person she's been so generous with—Kimiko works regularly into the single digits of the morning for clients, colleagues, and friends—and this is her thanks: a new life for me.

I HAVE BEEN IN HIROSHIMA for exactly fifteen days and at last the ground is under my feet. If it has not been as slow a start as I imagined, it has felt eternal. Tonight, I'll be sleeping on the floor on a futon barely thicker than a winter quilt. I will be writing in my own home. Tomorrow, I'll learn how to take out my own garbage. Kimiko is worried that it's too complicated, that I'll never remember which things go out on which days and how to wrap them, but she doesn't realize that I *want* to learn. I'm looking forward to taking out my own garbage, because that was Brian's job. Until I got here, I never realized that, in sharing our lives for so long, Brian and I each grew to excel in some things and to allow other talents to atrophy. If garbage removal doesn't seem like a talent, still I want to bag it, wrap it, tape it, and set my alarm to make sure it goes out sufficiently early on the right day.

And on the mornings when there is no garbage collection, what will I think when I open my eyes? Of course, I'll be doing my research, but still I imagine a morning when I might not have to get up at all. This wasn't possible in the hotels—too much transience—and before that? In all my thirty-seven years, as a daughter, a wife, and a mother, I've never had the luxury of waking with my eyes closed and thinking, without any recrimination or guilt, without any other person's needs to consider:

*What do I want to do today?*

## JULY 12, 2001

ON THE RIVER at low tide, in the rain, there is a small sampan swinging on a pole. The pole is about twenty-five feet long and bamboo, considerably longer than the boat or the man who leans his shoulder against it. He is standing, in a rain jacket and hat and a white towel tucked under the hat to protect his neck, in a soft warm rain on the wide, muddy river—he is leaning on water that sighs when the rain hits it but otherwise does not move. The boat and the man are equally still. They are worn, and veiled by rain and clothes and tarps and towels.

There is a black dog sitting in the bow of the boat.

Behind them, there's a bridge, weighed down with morning traffic. Miniature cars for the narrow street—minivans half the size I'm used to, narrow but high, like a single serving loaf of Wonder bread. They are lined up, stopped and yet revving with the energy of the day that's just beginning. They are going somewhere. You can feel it. The cars link the twin flanks of boxy, concrete apartment buildings that zigzag down each river bank. It's an uninspired landscape, if not downright ugly, and very much in opposition to the stereotype of Japanese "good taste" I keep hearing about; the stereotype that wrapping is everything and no one cares what's inside. And it would be easy to condemn them if you didn't know that every single structure in this area had been shattered and burned in 1945. Windows becoming scatter bombs, beams becoming guillotines, beds becoming funeral pyres. The remnants covered in ash, buried shortly by a new layer. This time of bodies. Flayed, ruptured bodies . . . bodies that survived for hours—powered mostly by shock and by habit—before falling wherever they stood.

Women, babies. People once.

And in the shallow river that they might have been heading for, the river that was once so full of people desperate for a deadly drink of water that you could walk across their bloated bodies to avoid the fevered bridge ties, there is now a man and a dog in a sampan.

Fishing for clams.

# PART II

## IN THE MORNING

*Some things have to be believed to be seen.*

—*Ralph Hodgson*

# |
# ON THE HILL
# |

**H**OW SIMPLE TO ERASE.
It starts with a small,
stubborn no, and Japan
could be its birthplace: here, they have perfected the barely
perceptible smile, the sliding maybe I've become so familiar
with. If I'm making inroads now, if I'm gaining trust, I am
still offered exactly what the person in front of me wants to
give. Buckets for washing myself; a memory of grasshoppers. In Japan, you can refuse a sweet and still be presented
with it, and with the great expectation of your satisfaction.

I have been invited to the headquarters of the Atomic
Bomb Casualty Commission, where there is tea in the
chairman's office and windows that slide open to look out
on a few well-placed shrubs. This is the organization that
Aunt Molly worked for, which launched my journey. It's
housed on the top of Hijiyama, the only hill in the delta
that is downtown Hiroshima, the hill that's most famous
for being the only shelter from the blast of the bomb. Now,
it is home to the organization that began as the first wave

of American medical researchers, home to their grey, tin, bisected cylinders—Twinkie barracks—which were erected in 1951 overlooking a sprawling, multilevel cemetery filled with war dead. The placement of these facilities, their purpose, their very existence, can cast a quiet cloud over the faces of the people I am interviewing. Now I hesitate to say that my aunt worked there, and hasten to add that, when Molly applied, she had no idea what they were doing.

Which was: measuring the power of their unknown weapon in the bodies of the wounded. Providing no treatment, withholding the results of the tests. Classifying research and disavowing any "significant" lingering effects or genetic mutations from the radiation.

I can't think of this place without the anger, the accusations, that accompanied my introduction to it. The ABCC were the people who tried to take your baby's body, who sent their car for you if you didn't report on your own to the doctor's office and gave you nothing in return. Their betrayal was not only in the fact that they had no intention of healing, but in the expectation that they were the doctors, and if there was no refuge in them, there was no refuge at all.

Except that, these are no longer the people. In 1975, the ABCC ceased to exist. It was replaced by the Radiation Effects Research Foundation, or RERF, which differs from its predecessor in that it more specifically sets out its identical mission—research, not medical treatment—and is directed jointly by the US and Japanese governments, which was claimed to have been the case all along. Same facilities, same staff when the progress of time is accounted for. These people are interested in my aunt, though none of them have ever heard of her. I tell them that Aunt Molly worked for one year as a file clerk or maybe in the statistics department in 1946 or 1947, when there were only twelve or fifteen people on the staff. I tell them the name of Molly's boss, and that she was bussed in from the nearby town of Kure. But somehow Aunt Molly neglected to tell *me*, until long after my visit, that she was known by her maiden name when she worked there, and that her first name was mispronounced as "Marie."

The name change will forever obscure my attempts to find her there.

Still, the ABCC staff—I think of them this way because I've never heard anyone off the hill refer to the RERF— are very nice. I'm escorted there by an energetic, mountain-climbing man who used to work for the Commission in the 1950s. The librarian turns out to be the very warm and helpful daughter of one of the women who escorted the Hiroshima Maidens, the disfigured girls my aunt first told me about, to the US for surgery. I am a writer on a grant from the two governments that fund this place, so I'm greeted by the chief of the director's office, by a representative from the general affairs section; I'm invited for a brief tea with the chairman himself. There is a private showing of a video presentation on the RERF and its research. Their entire organization, it seems, is open to me.

There is, among the staff, a slight reticence in talking about the past. They're excited about the research they've just begun on the effects of radiation on the children of the *hibakusha*, and also about the results of their more recent studies that show much higher rates of cancer in people who were exposed to the atomic bomb, as well as low-to-medium levels of exacerbation of many other kinds of illnesses. If the ABCC declared, in its first ten years, that there were no such effects, well, they are not the ABCC. Let us talk instead about Electron Spin Resonancing, and how RERF scientists are using it to measure doses of radiation and correlate chromosome aberration frequency in lymphocytes. The RERF contradicts the ABCC wholesale, without ever admitting that it is a contradiction. The mistakes, the manipulation, the evil if there was an evil, are simply gone.

MY MOTHER DOES NOT COME to me until I leave the compound and walk to where I'm standing now, on the edge of the road, looking out at the terraced military cemetery of war dead. I feel her, and wait, taking in the jumble of stone beneath me, wondering whether no one is visiting because it's too hot—which is the most often uttered comment I've heard so far in Japan—or because the families who would care for these graves perished in the bomb. I'm getting used to my mother's presence and fully expect that she's here to give me another puzzle. The last time she visited me, I was standing in front of the A-bomb Dome. There, she 'showed' me a white crane disappearing into the rubble. The bird took me back to my wedding, for which my mother's entire family folded one thousand white origami cranes for good luck. My grandmother had not been happy with the color—white for death, white for modern young people

88

in Hawaii—and I was still working out what my mother meant for the crane to tell me, other than that I should call home. I'd called—mother's orders after all—and it was a nice conversation. Brian was sleepy, he'd been out late to a concert the night before; he and the boys were going to a baseball game together later. These adventures had defused some of the testiness that had recently been creeping into our conversations. For the moment, all was calm.

I am also happier. I am settled in my apartment; I have a few friends, including Kimiko's small group of peace activists who invited me to a party on the riverbank on August 6, the anniversary of the bombing. The activists are a diverse group, some very political, others very religious; some *hibakusha* themselves and others just folks with time on their hands. Ami will join us. I don't know yet which category she fits into: she's a single woman, an only child living with her parents, so she has plenty of time to organize interviews for me, to translate them, to show me a bit of Japan. My freedom, not only my lack of daily duties but also the odd conclusions I often draw from the left field of being American, intrigue her, and she's begun taking me to see some of the traditional arts that are still practiced here, like Noh. She is watching for something in my reactions, an urgency, maybe, a sign that it matters; I can sense it but am trying not to shape my response accordingly. And if Brian is still not terribly interested in my activities, I choose not to dwell on that. At least he has pictures of my new apartment now to place me. Sometimes, I try to tell him about my interviews: the *hibakusha*'s insistence that they hold no grudge against

America for dropping the bomb and killing their families; their emphasis on their sacrifice and their duty, which is nothing less than to save the world. They have a strange idea of peace—they believe it exists *now*, that all we have to do is get rid of those nuclear weapons and there will never again be a war. It seems naïve—not because I'm against disarmament, but how do they disregard all the wars around the globe since the 1940s? I don't dwell on this with Brian, though; he switches off so easily.

Today, overlooking the cemetery, my mother is quiet. I know that, if I turn to see her, she'll disappear. It makes sense that I have no image to accompany my mother's presence. I imagine her as a soul curling up in the softness of her body, inhabiting less and less of the outer layers. It's a slow process: first the skin is not her own, then the fat. We know little about my mother's dementia and less about how it will progress; until she dies, we can't even be sure which one she has. The poet in me takes refuge in this, or perhaps it is the child, imagining that it's not my mother who is confused and losing, but interaction that has become too much work.

There is then and now for my mother, just as for the ABCC. *Then* I often locate in my late teens, when my mother and I used to eat Ritz crackers with cream cheese and mango chutney after school and talk about my day. I had an endless stream of friends who wanted in on those chat sessions, who wanted the kind of advice and comfort their own mothers couldn't give. My mother sparkled—so precise, so empathetic. So intelligent that no one could believe she hadn't finished college.

*Now* I am sworn to silence. There's a ban in my family against anyone knowing—my father's request, his worry that it will depress her if anyone says the wrong thing—and we honor it, even if it draws us inward as a family, as friends and colleagues see less and less of her so information doesn't leak. If it's lonely sometimes, it also means that I can forget, for stretches of time, that this is a death sentence. From far away, my mother is always healthy; the slips of mind, of memory, become an impossible dream. From far away, though, I can be lulled into turning toward my mother—for advice, a commingling that can no longer be had—until the small, stubborn "no" in my head reminds me that it's less painful to forget what I had with my mother than it is be reminded of what I've lost.

Perhaps it is the dead spilling down the hill below me, but suddenly, I'm in tears.

I am surrounded by lies. Tea and plants, a name change—these should be the poorest camouflage. It is more than the ABCC: I have a sheaf of claims that the group's mere existence is proof that the bombings of Hiroshima and Nagasaki were no more than experiments on human rats to see what these two new and different weapons could do. I've read proof that Roosevelt knew the Nazis had given up on their nuclear research before the Manhattan Project began, and that Japan had exhausted its manpower and weaponry by 1945 and was no longer a threat to America. There is compelling evidence that Japan was trying to surrender gracefully; that the US bombed Japan to gain advantage over Russia in the terms of surrender. That the top-secret meetings to select Japanese targets for the two A-bombs focused on a list of cities that were as untouched and self-contained as possible, so that the new weapons' powers could be accurately measured.

These facts have not been hard to find, either. And if competing theories have also been published, the enthusiasm for measurement—in site selection, in photos and surveying teams, and in a team of scientists to record the effect on living bodies for the last fifty-five years—seems to clinch the proof. Even if these facts are spun, if they are layered and reassembled, still no lies can change what happened. The bomb was dropped, many people died. And in that moment, Hiroshima became indelible. This is what the Peace Museum should be saying. For all its smiles, the RERF should be ashamed. Here in Hiroshima, at ground zero, there should be a grand purpose in getting these truths out there. But not even the *hibakusha* will talk to me about these things.

MAIDENS

It is 1955. Twenty-five young girls, bomb victims, "monstrous reptiles" as one will describe herself, are flown to Mount Sinai Hospital in New York for plastic surgery to reconstruct their faces, their fused fingers, to remove the thick, keloid growths that make it difficult for them to eat and sleep. These are the Hiroshima Maidens, the *gembaku otome*. The first girl to undergo surgery will die almost immediately on the table from complications from the anesthesia, the others will have multiple surgeries—twenty, thirty—which will take more than a year to complete. While they're in America, they'll visit many different places with the friends who are sponsoring them. They will go to Berkeley, heart of peace activism, where Aunt Molly lives.

Who are they?

THEY ARE THE GIRLS who were put away in a box for changing, for being in the wrong place at the wrong time and daring to survive. Who did they become once the bomb had fallen? Were they different on the inside or just a new face on an old body? Were they different again after they had been surgically reconstructed, or still the same—just with a new skin? I am preoccupied with this change. Does it go deep or is it all my imagination? Perhaps it's just a reflection of us, looking from the outside: of our compulsion to recognize, and our own fears.

TODAY, I SPOKE WITH one of these famous Maidens. She was fifteen years old when the bomb was dropped, and she remembers it like yesterday, she says. She tells me that her mother saved her life: first, by pulling her out of the wreckage only moments before the fires began; second, by foiling her repeated attempts at suicide; and finally, by exhorting her to live from her deathbed. Her story is very sure and complete, even though she waited thirty years, until her mother died, to begin telling it.

Yet it is the same story I read before I met her. I found many versions on the internet, but they all started in the same place, and varied mostly in how much or little the woman chose to emphasize her work for peace. I could see it unfolding, the three of us sitting for ninety minutes to transfer translated information that I already know.

People have told me I came too late, that I should have been here fifteen years ago when more of the *hibakusha* were still alive. All they have left to offer is an echo of what they said last week, last year; an echo of the first thing they recalled when they began to talk. Where is the anger? I asked Ami after our last interview. *How can they feel so little about what happened to them?*

I equate feeling with honesty. But this time, there are things I will not ask. What did this woman look like before the surgery? What couldn't she do? How did it feel? I don't want to be a voyeur. As much as I long to feel what they are feeling, I'm not convinced I need this information, and I know this woman doesn't want to be an object of pity.

She wants to be a savior.

So instead, I ask this Maiden something else—more polite, but still different—to draw her out of the usual form she inhabits, the codes she is used to, to discover something about her that she does not often present. I ask her how the mind remembers.

"Tell me about your mother," I say, smiling encouragement. "You said she saved you. What was she like?"

"**M**y mother?

"My mother worked all day. She worked as an office clerk, and then at a bar during the night. There were many bars and restaurants in Hiroshima for the army. She also worked on a construction site. I'm not sure of her age then. She was a small woman, and she looked young.

"No one has ever asked me about my mother.

"My father died when I was three, and my mother left me with a relative until I was six. I'm not sure of her age then either. She often came to see me. She didn't marry again for me. I think that, after my father's death, she wanted to put things in order. I don't know.

"She worked so hard the whole day through so that I could go to school. I did anything I could. I cooked the meals, I had to cook rice on a portable clay stove because we didn't have a kitchen range. I cooked *nikujaga*, and also curry rice. No, she didn't ever say whether it was good or not. We talked a lot while we were eating, but I don't remember what we talked about. I have very few memories about spending time with my mother. I do remember that I had to help her—she had so many hardships. But when you get to be five or six years old, all you want to do is play."

—Seventy-one-year-old Hiroshima Maiden

|

# SISTERS

|

THERE IS A WOMAN I wish I could talk to, dead now from breast cancer, only two years before I found her, needed her, before I stumbled onto her story in a book and thought, *yes, I need this life.* Irene Saeki was in her late teens and early twenties during the war; she and her younger sister Meg were Americans who went to live with their grandparents in Hiroshima toward the end of the 1930s for health reasons. When Pearl Harbor was attacked, she and Meg were separated from their parents and siblings in the United States, and so, as history picks and shuffles its cards, they were not sent to the internment camps with the rest of their family, but instead were in Hiroshima when the bomb fell.

Here is Irene. She speaks English. She is sitting in a top secret room, in a mansion in the Sentai gardens where the Japanese military is headquartered. She is one of about thirty American girls who have been forced to transcribe shortwave radio broadcasts from the allies for the Japanese army. It's not the kind of job a young girl talks about, so very few people have ever heard of this unit of "girl monitors," and no one seems to know who they were, or what the room looked like, or exactly what they were asked to do. But we know that there are three shifts of ten girls, and that on August 5, Irene is on the night shift, so she begins walking home an hour before the bomb instantly kills every girl on duty and also many of the girls who were on the night shift and had lingered in the building. She searches for her sister Meg in the rubble of the city, and in doing so, is exposed to high levels of radiation. Despite the bomb, despite the internment, she chooses to return to America as soon as possible. She, the most beautiful of the sisters, the one who always strived to be the best.

Here is Meg, the schoolgirl. The seventeen year old who was forced to work as a mobilized student about a mile away from the blast. She was knocked unconscious; helped, fainting, out of the building; she ran through the fires in river-soaked pants; she wanted to die when her hair fell out, when it felt like her very life was draining out of her ears, when, a year later, covered with scars, she couldn't bear to go outside. Two weeks after the explosion, when Meg was finally brought home by bicycle, her face and body were so swollen no one recognized her. She also left Japan, returned to America on her own as soon as she could travel.

In the meantime, their family in America had returned to Hiroshima. And the next youngest sister, the one who was in middle school in Fresno, the one who was sent to an internment camp in a swamp in Arkansas—plagued by sewage backups and malaria and home to four species of the deadliest snakes in the country—to keep America safe from spies and other potential enemy infiltration, is still here. She is, by stunning coincidence casually discovered just moments ago, the woman I am slurping udon with.

Jane Osada. The ex-boss of my mother-in-law's friend.

The thrill of petrified information, of Irene's world rising from the dead, is dashed when Jane tells me that her sisters never talked to her about what happened. Their experiences were too much to share, too full of the possibility of resentment, the unbearable specters of who was lucky and who was not. Meg is still alive in California, but neither she nor Jane know much about Irene's world during the war. Jane has never heard of the book from which I learned about her sisters' lives; in fact, I know more about her sisters' stories than she does. She can tell me only, ultimately, about herself.

So here is Jane: the lucky one. Sixteen, living in the wreckage of a country where she has so little command over the language she is not accepted into high school and is advised to go out and find work instead. She gets a job with an entertainment group that organizes tours across Japan for the Allied soldiers. It's a huge amount of responsibility for a teenage girl, and a freer and more exciting life than most Japanese women could imagine. She travels around the country with the entertainers, she marries and has children, and she then separates from her husband in a vague circumstance that my reeling mind does not probe. At some point, she sends her children to live with her parents while she works to support them all.

The visions, the versions, are splintering. Three now, with other, equally fascinating sisters, one who went on to create parts for rockets, still to come. I am grappling with their stories—the way they have been told, the way I imagine them. How could I have let so many stories vanish? So many lives that are essential for me to know?

What, I wonder, is the right question? What is the locus on which all these stories spin? Jane is Japanese American, someone who experienced both the camps, and on some level, the bombing. She is the second of these rare creatures I have found. Jane is available, and unlike Aunt Molly she remembers; she will tell me anything she *can* tell me. It's up to me to figure out what I need to know.

*Why did you stay here in Japan?* I ask at last. *Why did they return to America?* This is the crux of my novel: how do you choose who to be?

I wait while Jane considers her noodles. She takes her time. And then, at last, she gives me a small smile in apology.

"I don't know. Like I said, we never talked about it; we didn't want to dwell on the experience. It seemed like fate that one was here, and not the other.

"Where we were when the war began, that changed everything. It changed who we were. I didn't think about it, though, and I don't think they did either. I didn't plan to stay. It just happened that way."

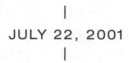

JULY 22, 2001

THE SOUND, when I close my eyes, has no Western consonance, tone, or rhythm—these are sounds that, if it's possible to describe them at all, are a kind of deciduous yodeling with random drum beats. Eyes open, I am watching men dressed in female masks and clothes sing in the bass register and dance with fans, flicking their toes up in the air when they move. I have never seen anything like this. But I have it on good authority that it's supposed to be beautiful.

I am spending four hours this afternoon watching a Noh performance. I don't know anything about it, and Ami doesn't either, though her father has been practicing it for fourteen years.

Here is a play that is unconcerned with narrative. There is very little language in the presentation, and even Ami, who has a copy of the text in her hand, says it's difficult for the average Japanese listener to understand since the words are at least five hundred years old and many are obsolete. Meaning may also be obscured by the delivery, which seems designed to mimic two people in scuba gear trying to have a conversation in eighty feet of water.

The stage is square and wooden—an open-air pavilion in our enclosed stadium-sized theater—with a fairly simple, traditional Japanese-style roof, and a long, covered walk-way to the left where the actors enter and leave through an ornate, draped curtain and a burst of drumming. There are three pine trees painted on the back wall. I don't know what they are supposed to represent—perhaps just pine trees, but every prop is so stylized that I can't be sure. There's a column in the front corner of the stage, holding up the roof, which keeps getting in the way of my view.

NOH IS . . . perhaps it resembles a Greek tragedy the most. There is a chorus, the *utai* singers, all of them men, in black silk kimono and grey *hakama*, who sit on their knees in *seiza* along the side of the stage looking sleepy for hours at a time; there are the musicians, one with a small drum in front of him, a second with a small drum, like a trussed hour glass, on his shoulder, the third with a sideways flute; there is a narrator who also acts in the story; and then there are between one and three other elaborately costumed characters who sway toward the audience and say a few incomprehensible things before dancing in a small circle with a fan when called upon. The costumes are draped and pinched and heavily layered. They include kimono and *hakama* and robe; hats, masks, belts, robes, socks. There is a young boy on stage whose robe flies off his shoulders like bird wings. The breast of his kimono is plump, the legs of his *hakama* propped out, beginning at the thigh in a sort of hoop skirt arrangement. He is wearing a tall, two dimensional black hat that looks like a fish fin. To keep him properly assembled, men periodically appear from a small door in the back left wall of the stage, fiddle with his clothing and then leave. He and they and every element on the Noh stage are not meant to exist in real space. Everything is symbolic.

People sleep through Noh; when the performance had barely begun, a woman beside me began snoring with quite a bit of gusto. Ami assures me that you're supposed to sleep during Noh, that that is, in fact, how the sound is designed. I accept that statement politely, but I don't believe a performance would be given as a sleeping aid. As far as understanding, I am still struggling, quite deeply into the day-long program, to identify some unique element or sound I can follow in lieu of a narrative, and to make descriptive analogies ("the flute sounds like . . . ," "the yodel reminds me of . . . ") that will reformat this experience into one my brain can read. It's my New York nature, I know—my list-making—and I know from experience here that it's useless. I am no closer to understanding, and perhaps farther away.

Somewhere around three p.m., I begin to nod off.

There is a boat. Three good guys getting into it. There is a demon brandishing his sword. Before I started dozing, all the dancers moved in precise, sometimes barely perceptible motions, so obscured by their costumes that I could see only a flick of toes, a wave of fan, so tight and tall and lost in their many collars that they could be puppets, but this demon stomps and jerks and runs about in jagged lines, which brings the audience and the whole stage to life. It might be the three drums, and the flute, and the chorus that suddenly seems to be singing full blast in a unison chant that shakes the floor of the theater. It might be the demon, so explosive and the antithesis of everything we have seen so far, who brings the other dancers' art into sharper focus. The long, slow day has lulled me away from my questions, and with my barriers unwittingly, sleepily down, the play has become a tableau that resonates. It seems that, if I can hold the urge for understanding at bay, then I can enjoy what's around me. But more than that, when I'm not trying to make sense of it, it somehow makes sense to me.

# YOUR FAMILY NEEDS YOU

I COULD SAY, again, *it makes no sense*, but that has been deemed beside the point. It makes no sense that now, after owning the building we've lived in equally for thirteen years, the couple who live downstairs wants to negate our contract and increase their share of the house while I am in Japan. It makes no sense that Brian is under siege, racing from the front door of the building up the stairs in the middle of the night to avoid the woman who used to be our friend, whose uncanny ability to be in the hallway whenever he comes home would seem to be tied to a homing beacon on his car.

This is an issue Brian would normally leave to me to negotiate. It would have been my role, my logic we called on, but my attempts to respond by email have only made the hostility worse. *Thirteen years . . . can't they wait six months?* I think, but I know better than to speak—everything I've said so far has just made Brian angry. He is the one who can't find peace in his own house; I am having a great time in Japan—not even doing any work by my own account—and here's yet another thing he has to deal with. I know Brian is the kind of person who absorbs anxiety, which may be the reason why our neighbors are pushing. When he told this woman he couldn't make any of these decisions without . . . me, she responded:

"Well, then, she's just going to have to come home."

IT'S NOT HIS DECLARATION, but he's reported it, which means that he wants me to hear it. If it was his statement, directly, I could respond: I'm not allowed to leave Japan; more than seven days out of country and my fellowship will be revoked. The choice could be spoken: my writing, my life, this chance for me that we agreed on versus someone else's fabricated urgency.

Time is different for me here. The time I have is short, immediate. Our house, on the other hand, does not have to be dealt with now, nor should it be; it is someone else's anxiety. I'm surprised at how obvious this is to me, and how settled I must be here to reject my role outright. If I were still living in the pressure of New York life, I might feel differently. If so, it's a fringe benefit that I don't get caught up. These are the things I tell myself without seeing how foreign their lives are from my perspective. How, even when I steel myself almost nightly to have this conversation, I am always somewhat surprised that the issue is still there.

Brian wants it to go away. He wants me to make it go away. This is more than his mantra; I can feel it. It crosses continents with a high whine, not the kind you can hear, or protest. Even though I've tried and failed, even though we both know I can do nothing long distance, we rehash the situation nightly, with me offering the kind of logic I would present to these people if only anyone would hear me, while Brian fumes on his bed sandwiched between our sons who are supposed to be watching twenty minutes of a relaxing children's video.

How can they be relaxed when he is yelling? How can

they then fall asleep? Why would they want to talk to me when my tiny voice is competing with Barney, and when it's that same tiny voice Daddy is yelling at? I've asked Brian if there isn't some way to restage the scene to encourage the boys to talk to me, but in his current frame of mind, the time difference is my problem.

*Let me say hello.*

I can hear the prodding in the background as Brian waves the phone. *Talk to your mother. She's on the phone now. Just say hello. Talk to your mother.* I can hear them negotiate: my older son wins, so my younger son gets on first.

*Hey, sweetheart, it's Mommy.*

He is fine. Nothing is new. This is his report, adorned with a lot of silent nodding. If it falls short of my hopes, of my expectation that I might chat with them, hear their stories of the day, I know this boy is three years old, and I would not have expected to chat with him if I was home. But still— and now I am the one wanting—there's a part of me that wishes that one of them could think up a just a single piece of news. I try to describe the food I've been eating, to see if I can gross him out, but he knows nothing of chicken liver on a stick. I tell him about the dog in the fisherman's boat on the river in front of my apartment, and the birds that perch on my small balcony, waiting for him. I've told him these things before, but he likes animals and it seems that is all we have in common. Repetition, I decide, can't be too bad.

*Don't forget I love you,* I remind him as he passes the phone to his brother. As I ready myself again to speak of the dog and the boat.

I AM A BAD MOTHER: this is what I'm being told. Or rather, my mother-in-law has adopted a recurring email sign off—*Your family needs you*—and Brian doesn't understand how I'm not miserable so far away. There's no question that I'm temporarily absent; no question that I'm less of a mother in Japan than I could be in New York. But in the growing gap between my notion of good motherhood and everyone else's, there is a question rising: what is a mother supposed to be?

Brian was the one who wanted to have children. He had endless strategies for teaching boys to throw a baseball, despite the fact that he didn't know if he would have boys, and that he didn't own a baseball. Still, I didn't know; I wasn't sure; it wasn't me, and when I tried to picture myself as a mother, I disappeared. I told him about my nightmares, about my failures as a babysitter, and the truth that I didn't think I even liked kids. We went back and forth and back again, with me unable to commit, until Brian removed every obstacle I could think up: he would do it all. He would be the primary caretaker if I would just have them. If I would agree to help him out sometimes, if he needed help.

That was our deal. And if, in the early days, I was needed constantly, it became both habit and comfortable. I turned out to have very definite ideas about the merits of home-made baby food, limitations on television, and whether boys should be encouraged to hate pink. I became a mother—that creature I couldn't visualize. And there was so much to mothering that Brian and I actually believed, for the entire first year of Dylan's life, that it was physically impossible for one parent to look after two children alone.

No one questioned that I loved my children then. In fact, those who knew me, and knew of our deal, marveled at my abrupt domesticity. But now that I'm in Japan, people around Brian seem dubious. When he tells me of the most recent friend or work colleague who called him a "saint" for taking care of his children, I add that person to his list, because, what else can I do? I can't assure him that he is, or remind him that that's what he said he'd do; I can't consider the underlying issues because opening myself to them is not harmless. I can already feel the soft silt of guilt that will come through that door.

I remember the space I floundered in when I first got to Japan, the writhing umbilical cord in my gut that said he was the only person in the world I could turn to; this is his version, then—of missing me. I've been in Japan a month, and it's all going according to plan, this is what I must remember. If I can convince him to ignore the house problem, find a way to help him view it through my perspective, the tension between us will ease. We once talked about him coming out for three months to spend time with me, so perhaps it won't be too long until they are here.

THIS IS THE WORLD of the umbrella. When I first got to Tokyo, it rained almost every day, and everywhere I looked, a stream of brightly colored domes: flowing out of the train stations, flooding the streets, trickling along the iris garden at the Meiji shrine in Harajuku. Here in Hiroshima, where it is getting quite hot and sticky, the streets are filled with sun umbrellas, and most of them are black. There must be a secret to explain this, but it's not coming through in translation. I can't help but recall that, when the atomic bomb exploded over Hiroshima, the people wearing white clothes were protected, but any dark-colored design, especially black, was incinerated, and left deep burns in patterns on the skin.

In the black umbrella, protection and target are one and the same.

I IMAGINE THE *hibakusha* everywhere. Of course, they are here—even with the immediate deaths and the lingering cancers, they are around me. But, with a past like Hiroshima's, I didn't expect this curious silence. It seems original: the descriptions I have read of the burning city emphasize it—babies with long shards of glass sticking out of their heads who do not even whimper; people with skin literally dripping from their bodies who move like ghosts. And even in those accounts that describe pain and panic, there's a quality of distance so great that it's as if someone turned off the sound and rubbed out all the color. The most compelling picture of Hiroshima is the one that has no voice: the reverse shadow that was burned into the stone step when the person sitting there was incinerated.

It is shadows I am thinking of. The past should cast a shadow on who we are now. If there is a puzzle, then here's another piece of it: my mother, who forgot that she was interned long before she began truly forgetting; my family, who never mentioned it, who hid the photographs, for whom to heal was to forget. I am the descendant of a group of people who built a wall down the center of their lives, between the internment and their future, and thrived on the disconnect. That silence came partly from embarrassment. They were interned, and released, and the experience wasn't terrible enough to complain about, especially in contrast to the other atrocities of the war. But there was something else too: they were asked to prove their American-ness. And so my cousins are all only half Japanese, like I am. All of us English-speaking, all of us pizza-eating, melting pot Americans.

If the internment wasn't terrible "enough," it was still shot with shame and difference. The only way to escape, to be safe, was to be what someone else wanted you to be. In the case of Hiroshima, this need to scour the face that we show the outside world, to clean up the city so that healing, not keloids, walks among us, has become a municipal obsession. I'm reminded of the Maiden I spoke with: even if the *hibakusha* are being eaten by cancer, they—we, none of us—

don't have to play the victim. It's not a question of optimism or pessimism, of strength or of vision. It is identity. Choice. If we don't want to appear wounded, then all we need to do is to present ourselves as untouched.

Now that I am in Japan, I'm beginning to sense this mechanism in myself: there is a distance, a small gap, between the neat labels I present on the outside, and the more turbulent urges I'm finding inside. This is nothing special, not the consequence of some hidden trauma, it's simply easy: the external persona quiets the questions. It's polite.

*How are you? I am fine.*

But in this sea of black umbrellas, there is something in me, a possibility teasing the edges of my thoughts, that wonders if this adaptation—this ability to reshape one's persona—isn't both a blessing and a curse? My own Japanese American family is proof that you can transform yourself so thoroughly you become the thing you appear to be. If you choose the wrong persona, though, who are you, and what are you left with then? If Brian's vision of me is not quite my own vision, is that just a simple misunderstanding born of the fact that we're apart? Am I changing, or was I never that person in the first place?

# LILY

"I AM SORRY they are dead," the director of the Peace Museum tells me, as if he himself killed the women I'm looking for. "But have you heard of a woman named Lily Onofrio? She was also in the internment camps and she's a *hibakusha*. We have some relics from her family in the museum."

*Lily Onofrio. Tule Lake.*

*Yes.*

"Lily Onofrio is in Hiroshima?"

"Her family used to live here. Her address is in California. But she comes back to Japan sometimes for treatment."

*A box of ashes tied to an old man's chest.*

Lily didn't want to go to Japan, isn't that what the story was? Or she changed her mind at the last minute. Lily's mother-in-law died in the camps, I remember. Her mother-in-law in the box.

I remember the anthology where I first read Lily's story, how her chapter was bisected by photographs. Lily was a young mother—her infant was sickly, almost died. She was separated from her husband and then sent, after the war, to Japan against her will. Lily's story was very much the story of Tule Lake, the camp for "traitors," and the internees who were labeled dissidents and moved there. It was about the tortures and the stockades and the shootings—the worst of the internment. My first book was about a different camp, one of the most peaceful ones. Was Hiroshima in the version of Lily's story I read so long ago? Did I gloss over it then too?

I have the book somewhere, back in Brooklyn. I can read it again, find out how much I've forgotten, how much I must remember in some unconscious stream in my brain.

Brian can send it to me.

"Yes, I've heard of Lily," I tell him. "I would be so grateful for her address."

## TOO LATE

IT IS TOO LATE for my mother to join me here. I can't shake that knowledge, the sense that I should have done this years ago so my mother could see Japan. It's not just that my writing is attached to her history, or that this country is the home of her first language. My impulse has always been to expand my mother's horizons, because her life in tiny town Hawaii seemed so small.

My mother took care of the children.

It was my self-appointed responsibility to do what she hadn't. To live the life that could be claimed vicariously; even when I knew my mother worried about some of the things I did, I also knew that she marveled when I accomplished them, when I was safe another day. That was my greatest success—to be alive and well somewhere else—and there were calls in the middle of the night to double check, every time the evening news reported that someone somewhere in another New York borough had been mugged. My parents managed to stretch an uneventful 1950s existence into a lifetime. They raised me in a place where children could spend an afternoon without adults, diving beneath the lips of underwater caverns, because somehow, in the lazy shelter of this barefoot world, it was not ever possible to be harmed. Crime was rare, because anonymity did not exist, and besides, it wasn't practical. Stolen cars turned up in a field of sugar cane once the tank was empty, because it was an island after all.

If it was odd that a woman who was so safe would worry so obsessively about her daughter, I imagined it was, in fact, the placid nature of my mother's life that left her unequipped to deal with even the possibility of danger. When I was in college, my parents used to come to the big city every summer to visit me, and I would show them around, showing off, completely forgetting that my father lived in Greenwich Village when he was in college, and that the first time I ever visited New York, as a young teenager, my parents took me there, and my mother and I buckled our purses onto the epaulets of our raincoats so we wouldn't be robbed. My parents, too, ignored the past and allowed me to be the worldly one.

In response, I honored my mother's fear.

For all my plucky posture, I lived in New York very carefully, triple checking whether or not I had my keys, was heading in the right direction on the subway; I bought a lock that featured a steel bar that went all the way into a hole in the floor when Brian and I moved into our first apartment so there was no way to force the door. If my mother's fear had no root, it had branches, and I lived with her scenarios in my head: being knocked over by a bicyclist, picked off in a drive-by shooting, cornered by a gang of boys. It was Brian who chose New York. I followed him because it was where he went to college; I stayed because it was where he got a job. When we were together, it was exciting, but alone, I was easily exhausted. I narrowed my parameters: became the kind of person who always took the same route because that was what I knew, what worked, and there was a comfort in knowing it intimately, down to the length of each traffic light and the name of the vendor selling stale donuts on the third corner. In that way, I survived.

Japan, and especially Hiroshima, is a place without threat. My mother could have moved here by herself, discovered her history on her own. There is no protection to organize, no peace to make, no responsibilities.

She would have loved it.

Time moves, Ami told me, from present to past. That's what the Buddha said. Here, I have time on my hands to remember, so it should be no surprise that I am moving into the past to linger there. My past is still the place where my mother is always there when I need her. When I think of my mother—a woman who never did something for herself instead of for me, who spent her life driving me to the store, sewing my prom dress, hugging me when I did something wrong—I can still feel how I demanded that; how I resented it; how I loved my mother entirely. Though I never brought myself to admit it, in all those years when I didn't want to be a mother, it was partly because I didn't want to be *my* mother. And yet, I've also always known I wouldn't have wanted her to be any other way.

|

## AUGUST 1, 2001

|

I REMEMBER A TIME—we were sitting together on my sofa in New York, me and Mom. We used to spend hours hanging out, "solving the world's problems" she used to call it, so it makes sense that it was just the two of us.

She was talking about children. Again. How her children were the joy of her life. She did more of that as I got older. She didn't say, *You're thirty now, you're getting old*, but she did say things like, *I would hate to see you lose your opportunity*.

It was a time in my life when things were going well. Brian and I had had some problems, but we were working them out—we were both working really hard—and I was finally exactly who I wanted to be. I'd quit my job and, for the first time since I was a teenager, I was writing. I was whitewater rafting. I was in love with my husband. I was happy.

This memory is real, if anything can be called real anymore. I didn't know how to explain myself to her. The life she lived, the family connections, the caretaking that she found important—I didn't want that. It was messy, too easy for me to get derailed. So I just told her. I told her what I had: there I was, thirty years old, finally an adult, finally empowered. I was building an identity for myself as a writer, adding a little strength, a little daring; my new life was set up exactly right. This is what I'd been looking for, what I worked toward. This is what I possessed, and I was going to keep it.

She looked confused at first, and then amused. "But sweetheart," she said, "your life isn't over. It's going to change. That's what life is. You can't hold onto things the way they are, even if you want it. It's always going to be different."

|

## PEACE NIGHT

|

ON THE EDGE of the Otagawa, some three feet below me, smooth stones embedded in a concrete bank slide into the river. I am sitting just north of the Aioibashi, the T-shaped bridge that rests on the crown of the Peace Park, which is said to have been the target for the atomic bomb. Over my head, tens of thousands of cellophane ties have been strung on long ropes across the river. There are hundreds of ropes, beginning from one point on the opposite bank and extending into the tops of the building on this side. In outline, they suggest a sail, though in practice, the cellophane merely traces the wind rather than catching it. I've been riding by them daily on my borrowed bicycle, watching them multiply over the last two weeks as the anniversary of the bombing approached, but now that the day is here, I still don't know what they mean.

It is perhaps ten o'clock at night on August 6, the anniversary of the atomic bombing. And these ties are flying up and away from me in the darkness, sometimes grey ghosts and sometimes glinting silver when the wind pulls them into the lights from the buildings and the full moon. On the flat black river in front of me is a flotilla of sampans and luxury boats, and of course, the kaleidoscopic paper lanterns.

They are small, square bags of brightly colored papers, maybe eight inches in diameter. They float on thin wooden crosses, lit with small wicks. Some ten thousand lanterns: yellow, purple, blue, red, pink, orange, green.

I arrived in the early evening, when the banks around the main launching platform resembled something of a carnival, with lines of people four deep and hours long. I floated with the crowds, watching the people around me break away to buy a lantern at any one of the many stalls on the banks; I watched them write their wishes on the paper, and the names of the people they wanted to remember, and then take them down to the water to be lit and sent on their way. I've been told that the lanterns are peculiar to this area of Japan, and are designed to console the souls of the dead, but I don't understand exactly how they are consoled. I've asked myself: Do the lanterns call these souls back from wherever they are to spend a day among the living? Or is the anniversary a time when the souls will roam anyway, and the lanterns offer reassurance and remembrance that allows them to rest for another year? And what of the light itself—does the flame stand for memory, or love, or is it a safe place for the souls to inhabit while they are visiting?

The questions will not let me rest. *Are we calling the souls to us, or tucking them back into bed? Is the ceremony for them, or is it for us?*

This being Japan, of course, there is never an answer. *What do the cellophane ties stand for? What's going on onstage? What was your mother like?* No matter how simple the information I am asking for is, or how I phrase any question; whether I give a slew of choices to select from or offer none at all, the response is invariably, "I don't know."

Tonight, I must ask: What if there is no answer? What if there is no lapse between cultures or problem with translation, but simply no key that unlocks the meaning behind all these "I don't knows"? I spent the evening with the peace activists at their lantern ceremony, the purpose of which I couldn't quite figure out. We were south of the main launching spot for the lanterns, and the tide was running north for the first time in sixty years because of the full moon and so the lanterns did not flow by our chosen spot, but it didn't seem to matter to anyone else. We put up our banner anyway. We ate *musubis* and drank green tea. I found out that Kimiko herself is a *hibakusha*; she was eight when the bomb was dropped, and she will tell me that story, *sometime, when you are ready.* Meet this Czech reporter, she said to me, and then I lost her. A guest from French Polynesia played Eric Clapton songs on a borrowed guitar as I waited to understand what I was just told, waited for the evening's agenda, and was finally forced to confront the possibility that that moment might be all there was.

It was just a song.

I came to Japan to ask questions, but the longer I stay, the more inappropriate that feels. It's not that my friends don't want to answer, it's more that it's never occurred to them to break an idea or an object down. When I try to analyze, it brings the moment to a halt and I'm left with nothing—no explanation, and no experience either. It's a bizarre world where questions obscure the answers, where they stymie forward motion rather than opening up a path, but that's the world where I've found myself. An *"ichigo ichi e"* world, as one of Ami's friends tried to explain to me. One time, one chance. Or, *it is what it is, and it might be important.* I must accept the moment I'm living in, embrace it entirely, then let it go so there's room for the next moment. Living in this way, the meaning of everything will become clear.

Or it won't.

MY MOTHER IS STANDING in the darkened hallway, one hand on the frame of the door to her bedroom, the light from that room illuminating part of her face. And on that face, tears, and terrible anger. Which day is this, and who was it who said the words that hang in the air and caused the explosion? *I told you three times already! Why can't you remember such a simple thing?* She knows she should remember, and that she does not, and she's terrified. But the outburst is terror too, and a plea, a hope against hope that this not remembering is stress, exhaustion, that she's being lazy and if she could just pay attention we would all be restored. No one wants what is happening. No one can bear it. It's a pain that cannot be borne. So we rush through it, through recrimination and apology; we rush to restore ignoring. My mother will come to lose that fear, and those will be days of greater harmony and also greater sorrow. She will come to a point of complacency, where she does not remember what she lost.

But in the half-light of the hallway and of memory, my mother's eyes are still bright.

THIS LATE, only a thin parade of lanterns meanders down the center of the river. From this distance, they are principally red and green and yellow, though I saw many different shades of blue being painted earlier; there's one group, all red, nestled together in a float. The water is still now, so the soft lights serve mostly as a setting for the sampans, which putter by, dark and full of unlighted lanterns that they have scooped out of the river in their cleaning sweep. In one cluster, a lantern has begun to burn.

What if I stop trying to define for a moment—if I let the ties be just ties, if the lanterns are only paper sacks? If I give up my questions and just sit, what do I see? The lights of Hiroshima, undulating in long lines along black water—a mirror, and maybe the inspiration for the flying ties overhead. The street car running across the T-bridge—a piece of the real world where people still need to get somewhere, a reminder of the trams and the people on them who turned into perfect charcoal statues on "that day." If I walked toward the bridge and out of the shelter of cellophane feathers, I would emerge from the darkness by the A-bomb Dome, which sits like a half-forgotten nightmare across from the Peace Park. It is the dome itself—the skeleton of the dome, a helmet, spiked and dangerous, that makes it an icon. Tonight, with the lighting from the ground, it will be a beacon. In the morning, it will shrink—after all, much of the building is missing—and sink into its embrace of enormous trees.

At this moment, the tide is beginning to turn.

I have slipped away from my friends' celebration to sit on the riverbank alone. I've moved from the discomfort of feeling I have too much space to actively seeking solitude—as much of it as possible. If I was asked—how do you define yourself?—I would have to think for a while. Once I would have said my identity is solid, settled somewhere half way across the world, and if I am finding it increasingly difficult to access at the moment, that doesn't mean it's disappeared.

And yet, every night, when I sit down to write, my laptop is hot and heavy, and there is obligation in my keyboard. Brian has a list of friends and family who complain about how bad I am at answering their emails. How is the food? they ask. Seen any temples? In fact, my correspondence is not so deplorable. If I wish Brian was more interested in my experiences, there are still a few friends who respond to my reports, who hear my thoughts and answer with their own, who comment on my mission, which is increasingly important to me, of finding history in the stones.

But in the great truth beyond fact—in my dreams, in the chaos of my daily language—the distance between me and most of them is growing.

*You are always going to be different.* My mother's words.

THERE IS A SMALL SET of stairs leading down to the water where I sit for a moment near a photographer and his enormous tripod. He's shooting a cluster of lanterns nudged together in the eddy near the bottom step. Looking right down into them, I can see drawings made by children, of and for the people they love. Judging from the pictures, I guess the children are about my son Ian's age, which means that the creators of this particular group of lanterns have been in bed for quite a while.

My own sons will be waking up now, or possibly walking to school. I've lost track of days—is it a weekend? Is it vacation? Of course, it's summer vacation, which opens the possibilities for what they're doing now. It's been six weeks since I left home, so conjuring their faces is easy. I can set them in their context—which is happiness, surrounded by family. I can see them at home. I can also imagine them here, looking at the lanterns, crouched beside me, my older son leaning back on his haunches with arms crossed, surveying from safety; my younger one in mid-leap, about to launch himself inadvertently into the water. I can feel the softness of his arm in my hand, the baby fat between my fingers. As we look, together, I can almost smell them.

*There is a sketch of a cat, Mommy. A sunny face labeled "Yuko." There is a plane and a bomb and a small fluffy cloud. Over there, a school of fish. Urchins and starfish.*

And there are words also, words that bump my heart, in their bubble block letters, a smiley face beneath them with pink spots on the cheeks: *NEVER REPEAT THE EVIL.*

"Amazing Grace," a hymn that was played at my parents' wedding and my own, is being piped over and over through a reed flute I cannot see. The unsung words float with the lanterns, and it's hard to imagine the day when the bomb dropped, when the banks were not neatly paved, when the spot where I'm now sitting was choked with bodies. I've been told that, of the thousands who were in this spot, only a single teacher and student survived, and both spent their first long night in the river surrounded by the dead.

But now the moon, which throws a light bright enough for me to write by; the ubiquitous cicadas; the cool of the evening—all of these things have brought peace. Earlier, at my friends' celebration, I was asked to say something about how the lanterns made me feel. I thought of saying something about the ghosts, but I couldn't because I had yet to see a lantern. Now, without an explanation to rely on, I am beginning to feel them.

They laugh in bright colors in the dancing candlelight. They cry together, arms holding each other upright.

They do seem consoled.

|

# VACATION

|

"MAYBE WHEN THIS IS ALL OVER, we should take a vacation," Brian says. "Go to China."

"China?"

"Or Vietnam. You like the beach. The kids like the
beach."

"Mmmm." I acknowledge his words with a sound that's
becoming more Japanese daily. It is midnight in New York,
and we're taking a quiet moment to plan our future. I conjure an image of my children playing in the surf on the
beaches in Hawaii. "Ian sounded a little sad last night when
I talked to him. Or not very talkative."

"He's fine. He's five. Phones are strange for kids. It's like
you're a ghost."

"Mmmm." I don't like the sound of that but I know what
he means. I am constantly having to say to my youngest,
"Honey, are you still there? Mommy can't hear you when
you nod you know. You have to make a noise." I switch
gears again, back to the point. "We could stay in Japan. Do
some exploring. I've barely seen it."

"Yeah, but you like the beach. Maybe we should go back
to Bali. The kids would like that."

"What about Kyushu?" I offer. "Remember that email I
sent you, with the link to those crazy mud baths? It will be
warm there. Or we could go north, to the *onsens* where the
monkeys come down to the outdoor baths."

"Monkeys?"

"I sent it last week, maybe the week before. Didn't you read it?"

Brian sighs. "I don't know. I'll look for it. It's at work. I don't always have time to read my email at work, especially those long things you send. That's why I need a vacation."

"Mmmm," I say again. I try to make it sound encouraging. Brian is tired. He's taking care of everything. "Let's take one then. I'd love to. Japan is more expensive than Bali, but we'd save on airfare. Did you look at the last links I sent you? You're going to love it here."

"I don't want to do mud baths," he says, getting ready to sign off. I can hear it in his voice: the conversation is over. "I want to go scuba diving. Now that's a real vacation. You like to scuba dive."

"There were no crematoriums after the bombing, so we took my brother-in-law's body to a small, nearby park. His oldest son went back to the farm where he had been evacuated to get some twigs and logs. We mixed the dry wood with green timber and lay it in the bottom of a hole dug in the park ground, then we put the body face down on a wooden doorframe over the firewood. I don't know why you face the body down, but that's what we were told to do. Once his body was covered with firewood, we surrounded it with sheets of tin roofing and lit the fire. It burns gradually—that's why you mix the green wood in, otherwise, the body doesn't burn completely.

"We waited the whole night—it takes one night to cremate a body—and in the morning, we took the children to gather up their father's bones. At a crematorium, they would have given us long chopsticks to pick through the bones, but we didn't have those so we stripped some of the bamboo lattice from inside the plaster walls and used that instead.

"I tell people today, if you can cremate a body, you can do anything."

—Seventy-eight-year-old female survivor

STOP BY YOUR ANCESTRAL GRAVEYARD. Pull the car over on the sidewalk—you won't be long. You'll need one thousand yen to buy a paper "lantern" to decorate the grave. White for someone who died this year, multicolored if your spirits need less guidance to find their way back to their world. The lanterns are six-sided, pyramid-like, buckets on a stick. Green, then magenta, then yellow, turquoise, red, and deep purple. Some are flecked in gold, all have something in kanji written on one panel; they have small horned tabs and accordion dangles, and there should be many at each gravestone, one for every visitor, every ancestor gone. When you have chosen one and tucked it in, neaten the sticks around the gravestone, get some water in a bucket and ladle it over the top of the stone to make sure your family is clean and not thirsty.

Pray, bow, and then, "let's go."

THIS BROKEN, IRRADIATED tombstone I am kneeling in front of is from a temple in Nakajima, one of ten temples in that perished town that was directly beneath the explosion; it was recovered very near the spot where the cenotaph in the Peace Park stands now. The priest who is standing beside me inherited that temple from his father, more in spirit, obviously, than in substance. He would like to think that his parents, their parishioners, his friends and neighbors, that all of them died instantly. He knows his sister—a fifteen-year-old student who was crushed in a nearby munitions factory—did not.

This is Ami's ancestral graveyard on her father's side. We've already stopped at the maternal family grave. Despite what I was told about long family pilgrimages by train to honor ancestors during Obon, there is no family here today. It's just me, and this quiet girl who's become my friend. All our actions have been quick and painless. We are on our way to have dinner at Ami's house—I'm the guest of the only child, and though I did not want to intrude, they are alone, and happy for the company.

But first, we have to pay our respects to the temple priest, Toshiro Ogura. Here I am, the white woman; we need to introduce her, assure him that she has a purpose here, a sponsor (the Japanese government!), that she is appropriate (and we thank goodness that she wore one of the two over-the-knee skirts she brought from New York for this "conservative" culture). And when Ogura-san finds out that I am writing about the atomic bombing, he shows me an incredible map, square yards of paper, labeled in kanji, of every building that used to stand in Nakajima. Here is where his temple used to be. Where his life was until he was twelve. Here is the lost city, the answer, a map like no other. This is how my own life turns when I least expect it, how Hiroshima is layered: death, tradition, dinner. This is how I get an invitation to come back again to see the map of what the pre-atomic world looked like. Sometime. When it's convenient. And then the priest's wife takes me back to the graveyard, to the mossy stones that were recovered from the ruins of the temple.

This is my fall to my knees.

My path to the frayed and broken tombstone on Obon.

"So, I say to people, 'You are stupid if you trust what those comfort women say about all that nonsense.' Those are false stories. I was there in Korea, so I know.

"Those Korean comfort women were gathered by Korean people who owned their own businesses. We had nothing to do with it. But we left them alone when they started telling all those false stories because it's so ridiculous. Some Japanese veterans admitted that what those Korean women say is true, but they are all stupid. They just want to get people's attention. The Nanjin Massacre is another false story made up by some Japanese.

"Korean comfort women wore Japanese kimono on purpose and pretended to be Japanese to get more customers. They were happy because they earned a lot of money like that. Japanese comfort women were more popular than Korean ones, of course, and so the Japanese ones could charge twice as much. I remember that those Korean comfort women were really happy doing their jobs. I wasn't interested in those women myself though.

"So what they're saying about us threatening them at gun point to become comfort women is totally false. It's nothing but ridiculous. That's why we don't take it seriously. And one other thing is, we Japanese believe that we don't really have to speak up to let the world know the truth. We know that the truth will come out in the end no matter what. So, we just let people say whatever they want to say. It's degrading to confront those Korean people.

"We all think that way."

—the Colonel

# THE COLONEL

HERE IS THE ANGER I've been looking for. He is full of it, of hatred even; the world is black and white to him. He is the only person who rejects the plot of my novel as irrelevant and wants me to write a different book. It is his life's mission to correct misinformation about the bombing, and he freely lists the people who've gotten "upset" when he has questioned their credibility, so of course I should expect him to question mine. He has very specific, detailed memories, but some of them, like his insistence that the Korean comfort women were happy businesswomen, or that the Nanjin Massacre is "another false story made up by some Japanese" are outrageous. And yet, he insists that he knows because he was there.

I am sitting in Kimiko's living room, surrounded by a small group of translators and peace activists who have gathered to hear the Colonel speak. This man may be one of the only people left alive who has information about the girl monitors who worked in the Army headquarters. He is close to eighty, though he could pass for twenty years younger—a dynamic, smooth-faced man with twinkling eyes behind heavy glasses and white hair, and even though this is supposed to be an interview, he is seated in a chair with everyone arrayed around him on the floor, and he wants to start at the beginning, no, he wants to start *before* the beginning. He wants to start in Nanjin, when the chief of a special unit to end the Sino-Japan war gave him permission to film a movie to "console the souls of the war dead." He wants to tell us that he's a perfectionist, the sort of twenty-six-year-old man who would make the soldiers redo their scenes over and over by flinging up his arms and yelling until they got it right. But first, he wants to inform everyone in the room that this writer is completely misinformed and misguided, and how lucky she is to have someone like him to set her straight.

There were no exchange ships between the US and Japan during the war, he tells me.

*Well, actually, there were two.*

There weren't any internees from the US camps in Hiroshima.

*Not many, but there were a few. I am still trying to find them.*

You have no sources, then. You have no proof.

*I do have the stories of several women from books and transcripts. Unfortunately, most of them are dead.*

It's stupid to write a book about people that no one knows anything about.


IT'S THE MOST interesting interview I have experienced so far. Except that he won't let me ask questions, and when I ask anyway, he won't answer them. And when Ami tries to do a simultaneous translation for me, he tells her to shut up. I smile at her when she cringes, to assure her it's okay, and since that smile would be required even if it wasn't okay, I add some extra attentiveness and hope that works for everyone concerned.

After two hours, he is done with his introduction of himself; he has rehashed the now-familiar theory that the US refused to allow Japan to keep its imperial family in the Potsdam agreement because it had a four billion dollar bomb it wanted to drop and it didn't want Japan to surrender before seeing what kind of damage the new weapon could inflict on Hiroshima; and he is backtracking into his life on the frontlines in New Guinea. I hazard a few questions about the novel that's daily getting hazier in my mind: does he remember the Sentai Gardens, where the military headquarters were, and where the Nisei girls were kept confined to follow the Allied broadcasts?

He will get to that later.

*I am so curious. I am hoping to include these girls in the novel. And of course we should take a break for lunch soon, and I have another appointment at 3:30 . . .*

No.

That's not acceptable. *He* is the one helping *me*. He will control what he says, and when I can leave. I am clearly ungrateful, so he will no longer speak to me. After pizza, he will talk about the Sentai Gardens, but no one will be allowed to translate. There is more, much more, on the topics of how the day will proceed from this moment forward and of my abysmal ingratitude—I can tell by the spit coming out with his words—but it is met with smiles and nods and absolute silence in English.

What can I get from this man who will not speak to me? What does he remember, what of it is true, and if it's not true, then what is it? If I cannot believe, or even understand, then I must find a way to listen to what he's *not* saying, and in what order, compared to the person I think he is. I have not yet abandoned questions—at least not in my interviews—but I've stopped trying to force people into the world I understand; I let them offer what they remember as the most important things they carry. These are their gifts to me, the keys; they are part of a personal narrative far more important than my questions. And if I must now allow a world to grow from the Colonel's silences, then I must ask:

So this man—this didactic, belligerent man—what is he telling me, really?

He can't bear the past. He wants to be a hero, he can't entertain any blame against any group he was associated with: the army, Japan. If he can brag about his ability to keep his head and direct the Akatsuki unit through their famous relief efforts amid the fires and atomic haze, then he can snatch something good out of the wreckage. He's not interested in memory, or in different perspectives, or even in the truth. He is forging his own identity, and no one else can refute him.

HERE IS A MAP. Move away the box of pizza. This is a map of the city as it looked just before the war. Over here was the military headquarters, here is where the Emperor and Empress used to sleep, and here the Sentai Gardens, where those girls that she wants to know about intercepted radio signals and propaganda from the Allies. Of course, it was close to the epicenter, and was completely burned, but look.

There is a small black and white photo of the mansion at Sentai on the back.

At our headquarters, there was a girl we called "Kikubo"—the mascot girl in the medical department. She was a sixteen-year-old student, and she was injured terribly in the blast. I had a niece, too, Kyoko Yoshimura, only thirteen years old. She was seven hundred meters away from ground zero, pulling down houses to clear the fire breaks with her classmates. Kyoko got home that night, but she died within a few hours.

You can't imagine what we saw: terrible deaths, miserable scenes. It was hell.

Is it 3:15 already? Then you can make a copy of this for her. It is a picture I drew of the day of the bombing. This is the basement of Honkawa elementary school, a baby sucking its dead mother's milk. It looked just like this. There is another one, of the survivors at Miyuki Bridge, in one of the books on the table. Please give me five more minutes to improve her understanding of this tremendous tragedy for Hiroshima.

She is lucky to have me to answer her questions.

*Yes, I am.*

# HOME

THE CLOUDS HAVE gone mad. Against the bright blue sky, clouds of every shape and size vie for my attention. There are streaming bubbles, cellophane lakes of haze, proud feathers, and the sharp, renaissance boils of cumulus—these last just the caps in a field of mushrooms, just the ghosts of motionless anger and old pain.

The blue is like nothing I've ever seen. Not turquoise, not royal, but some rich mixture of the two. It is now very hot, and the sun adds a molten, buttery sheen to the surface of things.

Some of that could be sweat.

Living alone, a stripped down life, I have returned to pen and paper. It is scratch and sketch, by nature undigested; I can put down whatever occurs to me without giving it a purpose. I am writing my days, not editing, sometimes not even finishing an entry if life carries me away from the page. *Grab what is fresh and put it away*—that's what Aunt Molly recently wrote to me. In the quiet, where I am getting acquainted with the company of my own voice, these little notes are part of my new dialogue. My book is changing. I am writing something else.

It's hard to imagine now that, in that old world, there was a time when Japan was just a word in an advertisement. I found it in a magazine—*a fellowship, a six month stipend*—I rejected that for being too long, but kept returning to the page. What made me fold the corner, what made me show it to Brian without comment? That disquiet in me—if now it seems that it was not only about the war or my project—it was still so slight then that I had my excuses in hand when Brian brushed them aside and told me to apply. Now I see that, having been given permission, I could not have refused. It would have meant admitting fear, dependency, locking the door to a cage whose bars I didn't even feel. And yet, when the secret door is revealed, who wouldn't want to open it? How lucky I was to have someone to urge me to step through.

It's been three months now, and I'm not homesick any longer. Not for New York, or for the US, those places I've lived in but never claimed. Hawaii was my home and not quite America. New York was never my choice—I moved there to be with a man who could not imagine living anywhere else, and I stayed because I could never name a place I needed as much as he needed New York. His business, his pace, outweighed my occasional yearning for peace and for the ocean; it was more practical, and so it was.

This place—Japan—is not mine either, but it's a fine place to sit and wait in, to wait, not for the new world to begin, but for all the expectations and needs and responsibilities of my old world to spin down.

I am changing—not because I don't belong, but because I can. Without identifying anything that was wrong with my life, any part of my persona that I've grown weary of, I am losing things. Like sarcasm. Like planning. Like fear. And it's not that I'm becoming Japanese, either. I'm not exchanging one projection for another. Somewhere, beneath the borrowed New York tempo, I am beginning to recover an even earlier lifetime—the barefoot girl, the child running through the pastures behind her house in Hawaii, writing bad poetry beside the waterfall, embraced by hills that look very much like the ones that surround Hiroshima. Her heart beats more slowly. She doesn't need to lead.

And above her, above me, there is a painter's dream, where time has no bearing. It is past and present, overlapping, until one *is* the other, and all logic is lost.

This is where the girl is now, enjoying the silence. It is where she waits for me to fall back beside her, back to the moment in my life where I can begin again and learn to leap. Solitude has led me back to the last time in my life when choice was not collective.

In the realm of memory, which could be now.

# PART III
# AFTER THE BOMB

*This is the season when*

*the dead branch and the green branch*

*are the same branch.*

—*Rumi*

# | |

**Tuesday, September 11, 2001**

**Time in Japan: 9:49 p.m.**

TELEPHONE TRANSCRIPT

"*Moshi, moshi . . .* "

"Rei? It's Ami. Am I calling too late?"

"No. What's up?"

"Well, I don't know. I mean, I'm fine, but I think something happened in New York. My father was watching TV and they said there was a plane crash . . . I'm not sure what happened."

"What did he say?"

"I don't know. It might have been two planes, the little ones, maybe they collided in mid-air, I don't know. Maybe it's nothing to worry about, but my dad . . . well, he said, 'Doesn't your friend, doesn't she live in New York?' so I thought . . . I don't know. Maybe I shouldn't have bothered you."

"No, that's okay. Thanks. Let me call home and find out. I'll let you know if it turns out to be anything . . . "

**Tuesday, September 11, 2001**
**Time in Japan: 9:51 p.m.**
TELEPHONE CALL TO NEW YORK

"Mom?"

"Yes?"

"It's me, Mom. Reiko."

"Oh, Reiko! Where are you?"

"I'm still in Japan. So, what's up over there?"

"Oh, you know, not much. How are you?"

[Sound of second phone being picked up.]

"Reiko? My God, how did you hear so fast? We just
hung up with Brian. He's on the Brooklyn Bridge. He saw the plane.
He said it was huge and he knew something
was wrong, and then, boom! He called to tell us to get Ian out of
school. That's where I'm going now. Talk to your mother . . . "

"Out of school?" [Second phone goes dead.] "Mom, are you there?"

"Hi. Reiko?"

"Are you okay?"

Your father said not to let Dylan near the TV so that's my job. It's so
great to see the boys."

"What's on the TV, Mom?"

"It's that jet that smashed into the World Trade Center. Isn't that why
you called?"

**Tuesday, September 11, 2001**
**Time in Japan: 11:28 p.m.**
TELEPHONE TRANSCRIPT

"Hi, Kimiko."

"Have you heard? Have you talked to your family?"

"Yeah, they're fine. My parents are visiting, so everyone's in New York. All accounted for."

"You should come over. I'm watching it on TV."

"Oh, God, no. Those newscasters and all their drama . . . . It's okay. Everyone's okay."

"Reiko, they attacked the Pentagon."

"What?"

"They're saying there are eleven planes still in the air. Maiko just called—her son is in New York and all the lines are down—she can't get through. You're lucky you did. Do you want me to come get you?"

"No, I—Eleven planes?"

"That's what they're saying."

"Who's . . . ?

"They just said hijackers. They don't say. You shouldn't be alone right now."

"Hijackers?"

"You really need to see this."

"I don't think . . . I mean, I'm . . . "

"Oh . . . ." [sound of phone being fumbled]

"Kimiko?"

[silence]

"I'm coming to get you."

"What? What happened?"

"The tower—"

"What? What tower?"

[silence]

"Kimiko? Are you there?"

| |

Date: Tuesday, September 11, 2001
To: undisclosed recipients
From: reirei
Subject: okay?

is everyone okay out there???

| |

Date: Tuesday, September 11, 2001
To: reirei
From: Lorrie
Subject: Re: okay?

all is well in harlem and its environs

HOW Hiroshima is this?

146

HOW MANY TIMES can I say, "what"? It's a statement now, no way to answer. Too many things that could not happen coming at me. Skyscrapers . . . do . . . not . . . fall.

Down.

Except that, I was watching it. Watching TV with Kimiko when the second tower fell. I thought it was another rerun—of the first tower, which I still didn't believe—except that, the running Japanese commentary out of the box, Kimiko's leaps to grab the essence of the meaning and turn it into English before the next shock arrived, these things, they couldn't seem to explain why there were no towers left. I was just coming in, maybe that's what it was; just coming off my bike, my five minute ride across the river, across the empty streets, to her apartment. It was normal—a ride I often take, a familiar route, a familiar entrance without the usual hello. I could have gotten there even more quickly after I promised her I would come, but I didn't know . . . So I stopped downstairs first, at the convenience store, drifting through the aisles alone, the cashier watching me in silence, finally choosing a bottle of sake and some chocolate because . . . I had to buy something, right?

In situations like this, though, what do you buy?

**Date: Thursday, September 13, 2001**
**To: reirei**
**From: Nathan**
**Subject: Day 2**

Sadness and exhaustion are the words to describe the second day
of this tragedy. New Yorkers are wandering the streets looking for
something to DO. This morning I went to St. Vincent's to volunteer but
there are no victims coming in. They asked for sandwich baggies and
saran wrap to send food to the relief workers. I went to a nearby store
and bought all the baggies they had.

I've spent most of the rest of the day down on the West Side Highway
which offers an unimpeded view of the rubble. We stood along
the street to cheer on the steady stream of National Guardsmen,
firefighters from all over the country, buses of rescue workers and
dump truck convoys as they headed down into the War Zone,
like soldiers going off to rescue our city. We waved for hours and
held up signs that said THANK YOU and OUR HEROES. Later the dump
trucks began returning, filled with the carcasses of cars and twisted
beams that were being carted off to barges somewhere uptown. I
met a woman from Battery Park City who had literally run from her
apartment with nothing but the clothes on her back as the towers fell
around her. She had to dodge body parts and an airplane tire before
getting to safety in the Village.

The test for all of us will not be getting through the initial attack, but
how we will try to move forward. Our IDs are checked each time we
cross Fourteenth Street like it is a border. Right now the wind has
shifted and the smell is getting stronger as the cloud blows over
the island instead of out to sea as it did yesterday. I'm thinking of
relocating for the night to a friend's uptown although the mayor is
saying the air is not toxic. I'll wait a bit and see. All New Yorkers are

gaining a great new respect for our controversial mayor and feel in good hands with him at the helm.

That's all for now. I'll keep you posted. Keep us in your thoughts.

n

|

## SEPTEMBER 13, 2001

|

I HAVE BEEN WAITING in my apartment for something to happen, for nothing to happen. It's so still here, in the silence; I can hide here, I can believe the dreams of yesterday are just that. I will wake up, and if I don't wake up, I will be passed over, unharmed, just as I imagine that my family will be safe in our house if they stay inside and wait. I have friends in New York who are venturing out, searching the wreckage, roaming the ruined city. Except, it is not exactly ruined. They are fine, seem safe. They are snatching life from the debris.

New York is not Hiroshima. The world is safer if New York is not Hiroshima. Not a ruin where it was impossible to sightsee in the first stunned months, impossible to visit the epicenter as a tourist from a place of safety and normalcy for years.

Still, I imagine that my family is inside, like I am, all of us in the closet in the dark, waiting for the footsteps to fade, waiting until there are no more planes in the air—it seems, now, that there are no planes in the air. There is no word— no news, no more threats, no explanation or assurance to coax us out of this nothingness, this refuge where grief cannot move through the vacuum. Not yet.

There is nothing to do yet. I don't have anything to jump at, like Nathan, no way to move to prove that I'm not dead. Of course, I am not dead. My home is raining pieces of paper and bits of fiberglass and I'm not even affected.

I am the only person left on the planet who has no experience of war.


|

## SEPTEMBER 13, 2001

|


THE CALLS HAVE BEEN COMING steadily, into the silence. One of Kimiko's friends, Maiko, calls at ten a.m. Her son is in New York and she still hasn't been able to get through to him. She wants to know how I am. She wants to know if she should cancel the interview she's arranged with Dr. Fujita this afternoon.

Cancel the interview?

What is today?

I have an interview.

I have been up for hours; I am showered, dressed. I have nothing to do but sit by the phone, knowing that it cannot be Brian and wondering if perhaps it might be. Nothing to do but write in my diary. I haven't eaten; I haven't looked at my calendar.

Will anyone mind if I don't cancel my interview?

I have been waiting to speak with Keiko Fujita since I arrived in Hiroshima. She was a practicing doctor in Hiroshima during the war—one of the few still alive. I am writing a doctor into the novel, so I need Dr. Fujita's information.

Need is enough, I know. Fulfilling an obligation in Japan is enough reason, enough excuse to go out. But the fact is, I *want* to talk to her. I want to talk to someone. I want my life to move again, more recognizably, more truthfully than the sound of my voice on the telephone saying: "Yes, I heard. Everyone is fine. Yes, it's lucky isn't it? No, don't worry."

But Maiko's son is in New York.

"Hmm," I say. "What do you think? Perhaps it's not a good time for you?"

"No problem," she says. "I am fine."

Keiko Fujita has not just the promised two, but a full four hours of energy to give me. She has been telling her story, and helping others tell theirs, for decades, so she has more versions than I'm used to, with more details. Since she was badly injured in the bombing, she can't report on the hospitals, but she's delighted to go off the track and gossip about the colleague who stole her lunch in the waning days of starvation before the bombing; about husbands and families; about how she made a choice to care for her mother instead of being married; about wedding hairstyles; about hats. For the first time during one of my interviews, there is no need to keep her talking or press for details. Either she has an incredible memory or something has opened in her today. But today, there's nothing for me to do, nothing but listen, but watch. Amid these anecdotes are vivid descriptions of her wounds, her back sliced open, of the blackened post-bomb rush to get out of the city—some of the most powerful, certainly the most personal, descriptions I have ever heard. I feel myself relaxing as she talks, though I had no sensation that I was not relaxed before. Perhaps it's that I have found myself doing what I was doing before the World Trade Center fell, something I know. Perhaps it is that the narrative of Hiroshima is now familiar, soothing in its utter destruction, so much worse than now. The emotional blanks of Hiroshima have suddenly become reassuring: if Hiroshima is too terrible to be reexperienced, even from the distance of time, if it cannot be described, then it is intangible, just a nightmare. Something too aberrant to be repeated.

When Dr. Fujita is finished and has passed on other people's tales of horror, it must merely be politeness, then, that turns her attention to how awful the terrorist attack was and how happy she is that my family survived.

She makes no relative judgment between the two, so I am compelled to. What happened to her, I point out, and to Hiroshima, was a hundred times worse. An entire city, an entire network of roads, shelter, medicine, families destroyed vs. downtown Manhattan cordoned off but with email access and intermittent telephone. I tell her of the stream of messages I've received from every friend and acquaintance in my address book: *"We are fine." "Family Flood is safe." "It is very, very weird here." "I have a cold."* Everyone alive, home, safe. Some even with humor intact. Brian wrote to me about the guy who called his office several hours after the attack to rant about the rat running around his apartment.

But in Dr. Fujita's eyes, there is a break in the timeline, a union of past, present, and future. And it doesn't lessen her sorrow.

Her sorrow for me.

"I was looking at the airplane from the window and wondering whether I should leave home or not. Then, I felt as if my back was being sliced open with a sword. I couldn't walk, my leg was cut, my face was bleeding.

"One of the X-ray technicians who I worked with came to my house to rescue me. They prepared a stretcher. It was so painful, and then something happened, the string broke on the stretcher and I fell to the ground. I was in so much pain, so I stayed in the field for a while. Of course, there was no shade at all. I didn't drink—no water. I stayed in the open air.

"While I was lying on the ground, a woman came up to me carrying a stone—a large mortar. She put it down on the ground beside me, and then she died. I don't know why she was carrying the mortar. During the war time, we had such a food shortage, so maybe it was very precious to her. In the face of such a crisis, who can say how a human being will react? That woman picked up a heavy stone and carried it, and then she died."

—Eighty-nine-year-old female survivor, doctor

"We knew the world would not be the same: a few people laughed, a few people cried, most people were silent. I remembered the line from the Hindu scripture, the Bhagavad Gita. Vishnu is trying to persuade the Prince that he should do his duty and, to impress him, takes on his multi-armed form and says, 'Now I am become Death, the destroyer of worlds.' I suppose we all thought that one way or another."

—J. Robert Oppenheimer, recalling the reaction
at Los Alamos after seeing the Trinity Test—
the first explosion of an atomic bomb

WHAT IF, INSTEAD OF PLANES, they had used nuclear weapons? My parents, children, my husband would all be dead. My friends would be dead. Everything I own, everything I know, would be gone in an instant.

Just as the *hibakusha* have described.

This "instant" is where my head is now. I have known, intellectually for a while that, from the instant the bomb was dropped, the world was never the same. Not only crushed, not only gone, but also threatened by the very weapon we created. If anger brought me to Hiroshima, and if that anger was based in fear, then I am beginning to understand why I'm frightened. It's impossible to know *anything* about the bomb and not be frightened. The less you know, the more the gaps terrify you. The more you know, the more difficult it is to sleep. It's this haunting that my Aunty Molly passed on to me. It is not so much the effects of the atomic bomb that we have no protection against. It is, as one of the creators of that bomb once said, its mere existence.

And now, in the middle of a new attack, I realize that the possibility of war, the possibility of terror, has been with us all along. Why didn't we see it? Why couldn't we all feel it, in enough time to face it, in enough time—how naïve am I?—to stop it? What must it have been like to see it happening, to see the bomb dropping and have the time to wonder—just as Brian did when he saw the hijacked plane, too low amid the buildings in front of him, and realized something was not right? So there is that moment, then; the last breath of *before*: when life is about to change, utterly and forever, into something we have no way to conceive of. When the trajectory is already being drawn and there is no way to stop it.

Have we been living in that moment all along?

And when does *after* begin? In Hiroshima, there were thousands of people who were trapped in the rubble as the fires approached after the bomb itself had fallen; in New York, there were thousands of people who were hijacked in the air, or trapped in elevators or in their offices, with the full knowledge that there was no escape, that they were dying, that there was *not enough time*. And there were those of us who couldn't get through, who didn't know what was going on. Those who will retrace the steps that left us alive, that led our loved ones to the wrong place and the wrong time, who will finger our scars, the smooth skin where our ear used to be, and wonder if we should feel blessed or guilty.

This is the *hibakusha* twilight, the uncertainty that even the strongest of them dwell in today.

"My brother and I had no clothes on. Our feet were bare, and the ground was so hot that the soles of our feet burned and our skin stuck to the soil. I carried my infant sister on my back, and my father carried my mother, so our pace was very slow. Still, we made a desperate effort to get out of the burned area, which stretched as far as my eyes could see. The water pipes were broken everywhere, and near them, the dead bodies of people who had come for one last drink of water were piled on top of each other, crawling with maggots. There were half-burned bodies under the crushed houses. I made such a great effort not to step on those bodies, but there were too many. This is one memory I shall have to carry all through my life. I was eight years old then, but still now, after more than fifty years, the soles of my feet ache when summer comes."

—Sixty-four-year-old female survivor

Date: Friday, September 14, 2001
To: reirei
From: Brian
Subject: Re: Fwd: Returned mail: Cannot send message within
3 days

Hey,

Bush is coming to town. What the fuck do we need him for? He
says he wants to hug people. Can you imagine? The kids are back
in school. Mike was digging yesterday. He said it is far worse than
anything they show in the media. Took me two and a half hours to get
home last night with the car.

Slept like shit last night. Thunderstorms are running through town.
Must be miserable digging today. They pulled five guys out yesterday
though, in an SUV.

Running out of milk at the delis in the neighborhood. I feel alone
despite all the people around me. The office is quiet as hell. I'm here
earlier than usual, though. There was police action in the train this
morning. Kind of weird. About six cops got on and looked around.
People are obviously edgier than usual.

I continue to love you despite everything.

B.

| |

**Date: Saturday, September 15, 2001**
**To: Brian**
**From: reirei**
**Subject: Re: Fwd: Returned mail: Cannot send message within**
**3 days**

they pulled five guys out alive?

i feel very alone here too. i know it can't compare to what you are going through. here, i have shifted in status from "different because i am american" to "different because of tragedy." even though technically, i have no tragedy.

i would love to hold you, i would love to have you in my sight and know that you are safe. i keep thinking we should get the hell out of new york and go back to hawaii. live a simpler life together, the kind i am living here.

i have been loving you always. "despite it all" you say? because of it all, i say.

always.

r

| |

**Date: Saturday, September 15, 2001**
**To: undisclosed recipients**
**From: Karen**
**Subject: great article**

For those of you who didn't see it, great article in Wednesday's *Miami Herald* . . . click on the link, but here's a taste:

"You've bloodied us as we have never been bloodied before. But there's a gulf of difference between making us bloody and making us fall.

"This is the lesson Japan was taught to its bitter sorrow the last time anyone hit us this hard, the last time anyone brought us such abrupt and monumental pain.

"When roused, we are righteous in our outrage, terrible in our force.

"When provoked by this level of barbarism, we will bear any suffering, pay any cost, go to any length, in the pursuit of justice.'"I tell you this without fear of contradiction. I know my people, as you, I think, do not. What I know reassures me. It also causes me to tremble with dread of the future."

|

# SEPTEMBER 16, 2001

|

WE ARE TALKING ABOUT nuclear war here. The *Miami Herald* is talking about nuclear war. The peace activists raised the possibility immediately, but when I tell Brian, he thinks I am nuts with the same speed.

*Nuclear war? For Christ's sake. We're not going to drop a bomb on anyone.*

It's where I am living, I know, but even though this is the right statement, the best statement, it's also the most ridiculous thing I have heard since I left home.

One of the boys is refusing to go to school, Brian tells me

when it's clear I'm not responding. He's been banging his head on the wall.

I can still hear my son saying, *Mommy, a big plane came and crashed the Twin Towers. There was paper all over the school yard. It is very sad.* I can still see Brian's email: "[He] told me not to speak about the WTC yesterday cause it would make him cry . . . Dunno where that came from."

I have my theories, but Brian has other ideas. He thinks my children's mommy has been away too long.

*Why don't you guys come to Japan now?* I ask him. *In case there's another attack? Or a war?*

*Forget it. What would we do there? Sit in your apartment and hide?*

What else can I offer? What else to say when two of the tallest buildings in the world can collapse in ten seconds flat? I can't say, *Why don't you go to Barnes and Noble and get a book on how to help children who are worried about war?* Brian saw the plane through the slats of the Brooklyn Bridge. He was there, yards away, before any of the relief workers. The events I saw on the television unfolded over his head. Wasn't this, at least, something we shared?

Yes, I think, let's sit in my apartment. Let's stop. Hold hands. Be together here, where it's safe.

*Forget it*, he says again in my silence. *We'll be fine.*

I was searching for war when I came to Japan. How stupid to be searching for war. How strange that in Brian's mind, now, war is not the subject. Perhaps he's right: there is no one to declare war on. Terrorism is an act; it is improvised, isolated, and singular. The future does not involve nations, or armies, or arsenals.

A-bombs are a thing of the past.

But here in Japan, in Hiroshima, we are waiting. There is a sense that, from the moment the bomb was dropped, we have simply been holding off the end of the world. And we are about to lose our grip.

"Why didn't I die in the A-bomb?

"Why didn't I die?

"I was just a mile away from the hypocenter, Tenma-cho, working at a cannon factory. I was about fifteen at the time. My maternal grandfather and my aunt were at about the same location; they were living nearby so they were also exposed to the A-bomb. The only difference, they stayed overnight in Hiroshima City and then came to our country house. I only stayed a few hours in the city after the bomb. The following day, I went into the city again to look for my grandfather and my aunt. I couldn't find them, so I came back. They were there—they looked so good. No burns, no nothing.

"And then . . . two weeks later, my grandfather died. Three weeks later, my aunt died. Because of the aftereffects. And a month later, I was almost dying; we never knew what it was.

"But coming to think of it, maybe that overnight stay in the city made all the difference."

—Seventy-one-year-old male survivor

Date: Tuesday, September 18, 2001
Subject: DAY 5&6
To: reirei
From: Nathan

Today, lower part of Manhattan was open for the first time. My friend
Cindy and I took our bikes down to Little Italy and Chinatown, which
were bustling with newly re-opened shops and markets. We made
it all the way to Battery Park where the smoke became quite heavy
and we realized the wet streets were not from the rain but from the
massive cleanup effort. We never got to Wall Street because of
blockades manned by the national guard who asked for ID, but we
were able to see a lot of the debris and damage and connect with
fellow New Yorkers who were piling out of the subways in droves to
see what they could see.

Some of the images I won't forget include the group of people on the
edge of Battery Park holding cardboard signs with their addresses
scrawled on them hoping for someone to escort them behind the
blockades to their homes; Trinity church obscured by smoke but
standing tall; the burned skeleton of the Tower at the end of Church
Street with the smoldering pit behind it; the ASPCA rescuing tons of
pets from apartments behind the barricades; and, most creepy, the
two flattened cars parked along the side of the street . . . flattened to
about two feet tall, covered in dust and debris as well as flowers that
people had put on them as a memorial.

As we rode back up to the Village, it seemed Manhattan was getting
back to normal. People shopping, eating at outdoor cafes and being
New Yorkers on Saturday. Only the occasional emergency vehicle
to remind us of the permanent change that has taken place in our

city. Tonight my friend Chris and I went to a movie to do something "normal" and to laugh and forget. We found the perfect film . . . a movie from Thailand, a true story!, about a volleyball team made up of drag queens who ended up winning the country's championship match. Hysterical!

Luv,

n

"The black market sprung up around Hiroshima station. It was a sprawling mess. Shacks and tables, and everyone yelling, 'Buy this! It's cheap—get some!' Everyone was in the same boat. Everyone was filthy, buyers and sellers. There were orphans polishing shoes there. For the occupation soldiers.

"There was food, yes, but it was dirty. I do remember meat, dog meat, being sold. At least that's what everyone said it was. The taste was bad but we couldn't get regular meat so people ate a reddish kind of dog. I don't think they were pets—nobody had pets at the time. So we must have been eating wild dogs.

"There were other black markets too. There was one around Eibashi bridge, right next to the ruins of a burnt out house. Even now, I can remember it clear as day. There were bodies inside the house, frozen in position right in the middle of breakfast. Two people turned to ashes, charred black, just like that. They had been left there, and people walked by. When we saw them . . . why didn't we do anything? What did we think? Well, the bomb had numbed hearts and our brains . . . "

—Seventy-two-year-old female survivor

AMI SAYS IT IS SURE NOW that Bush is going to declare war on Afghanistan. She says ninety percent of Americans support war.

Afghanistan? A country? The home of already devastated citizens who had nothing to do with the attack? When I call Brian and begin to rant, my left-wing, nonconfrontational husband says, "Well, they can't just expect us to do nothing."

I wait. He doesn't retract it.

This is the man who wanted to join the Peace Corps. Who says, every Thanksgiving, that we should be serving food in a soup kitchen on the Bowery. Who cannot kill anything bigger than a cockroach. This is the son of a high school teacher who has the soul of a parish priest.

This *was* the man.

In the silence, I can hear his words repeat, exactly, with the same lift and toss, the same fall. *They. Us. Do.* It's the kind of statement that loops, disembodied, on a playback button: it will never fade, never soften; it can never be explained.

In the face of such a crisis, Dr. Fujita wondered, who can say how a human being will react?

*For Christ's sake*, he said to me—was it only days ago? *We're not going to drop a bomb on anyone.*

What does he know that I don't know? In what scenario is this retribution okay? One of my own aunts is forwarding me hate-filled op-eds, and when I try to write my own op-ed about this opportunity for empathy and self-reflection, my agent tells me I am out of touch and flatly refuses to send it out. Far better for us to kill them, because their friends might have tried to kill us. Before they can act again, before they think of acting, because they are weak, unaware. In a far off place, in a foreign country, small children dance to the news of September 11 while my friends wrap their grief and their sandwiches in cellophane.

Kill Mowgli, before he can grow into a man.

A rift has opened—between me and Brian, me and my country—that I've been trying to ignore. It's as if I'm watching the tower fall again: always seeing, never understanding, never believing, unable to accept. I would like to accept, intellectually; I would like to do something more than look on in horror, but my gut does not allow my brain to function. How, in this world that makes no sense, can we make requests of each other? How can we share our feelings when we don't know what we feel? Any development in Brian's life is nothing in the face of terror, and any report from mine is too fortunate. And though we say almost nothing in our daily conversations, still misunderstandings trip us. We try to stand up, brush ourselves off, toss each small, stubborn obstacle away, but they are everywhere. He doesn't see the world the way I do.

We no longer live in the same world.

**Date: Thursday, September 27, 2001**
**To: reirei**
**From: Lorrie**
**Subject: YAWN**

[That would be the sound of deafening boredom crashing around my ears. . . .]

So WHAT'S UP OVER THERE??????????

L

# PART IV
# LIKE A DREAM

*Doubt is not*

*a pleasant condition, but*

*certainty is absurd.*

*—Voltaire*

|

## RUNNING

|

I HAVE BEEN OUT. No longer inside, hiding; no longer whispering my worries in my head, voicing them to Brian who will not listen. I've been plucked off the ground—running from interview to interview to bar. If I'm not home, I don't have to answer the midnight calls from well-meaning friends about anthrax. If I'm out, pumping more alcohol into proper Japanese women than they have ever drunk before, I'm in a world where people will reveal themselves; they will confess to me, worry, ask me questions I can answer; they will give in to me, race down the center of deserted streets on their bicycles in the early morning. Here I am, wind in my hair of my own making. Behind me, a whoop of warning that my companion is gaining inches.

Behind me, white poison, and unease about where the next envelopes will be mailed.

*Do you want to come to Japan now?* I ask Brian again. *Maybe now, with the anthrax . . .*

He scoffs into the phone, and then lets the sound sink beneath the careful calm we've been trying so hard to create. Even though we have not stated it so baldly, the camel that was our life together, which had always seemed infinitely hardy, has become so burdened we're afraid to add to the load. I have ranted at him, in my own cloaked terror at not being able to recognize—not him, not my city—I am navigating by old snapshots of before. He has dismissed me: I *have no idea*. This is his mantra, this and the fact that he is *waiting for this to be over*. These are the gates we must pass through every time we pick up the phone.

In the chasm between us, black and white are beginning to edge each other, and the flexible grey that was our life together no longer has the strength to lead us through.

While we are gathering ourselves, waiting for the echoes to fade, he does *not* ask me whether I want to come home. This omission is immediately obvious, and all the louder for remaining unsaid. Am I being judged on my inability to get on an airplane to return to the center of the storm? I jump to this, read threat into it because that's how we communicate. If he asks, then he will be responsible for my loss of my fellowship; if I offer, the choice is mine. His silence is my chance to give up my life here, to choose him and the web that has always supported me.

This is my old world, the one I excelled in: of "shoulds" and "supposed tos"; of definitions and absolutes ready to jump on any offered word. The questions, refusals, agreements, counter responses—the permutations have a calculus of their own, with volumes and surface areas that change depending on who says what, who says it first, on the exact formula of the sentences. But none of the equations are harmless.

He is waiting for me to respond.

*The children* . . . but that's a vague start. I would interject: *you can bring them here where it's safe*. And he would finish: *. . . are fine*.

Death is a crapshoot. It doesn't matter where you are.

It appears, on the silent surface, that we're in perfect agreement. We are struggling to see the war as "not a big deal"—each one continuing to live a life, equally, separately, in the way we once agreed. The anthrax is nothing; it is not connected. In the space where there are no answers, it is better to pretend it's not happening at all.

If I once thought my trip would be easier on him in his own environment, it is now easier for me in some ways, because I can fill my head with another war, with the question of war, its nature, philosophy, with its broad history that has nothing at all to do with us, and little to do with what he's feeling. If only he would tell me what he was feeling, if only he knew. He will not admit to injury, and neither of us imagines that I might also be hurt. All our conversations are now edged, but there's nothing personal in our talk of the war. I am delving into the feelings and fears of other people, a subject that he is emphatically not interested in, and when I ask him a direct question about his own feelings and fears, I cannot shake the story that he's okay. That he's "ignoring things mostly."

I don't ask which "things." Nor do I turn the question

on myself. Although I would never admit to ignoring anything, I am the grand suppressor: an emotion rises, pokes up its crown, and before I can see its face—before the eyes can tell me I am hurt that he won't come, that he makes fun of my fears and has never once tried to find something in Japan he might love in the extensive time he could have given himself here and chose not to; before the lips can say that I've changed, without intention, and do not want to be sucked back into my old life before I can understand what my new self looks like—I push it back down. I have never been strong enough to reject a direct request, especially from my husband. And if I have gained that strength in his absence, if I have my own stake in his denial, neither one of us is prepared to know.

*Don't go to the World Series*, I beg him. *Something could happen there.*

He has tickets.

I stay in Japan.

I want to be in the company of the *hibakusha*—because they have seen the worst and will recognize the end when it is coming while the rest of the world watches, as dumb and disbelieving as we were the first time. I don't know why this is so important to me exactly, except that the clock can't be turned back, nor can it go forward, nor can I find any reason for it to stop here, any reason for any of us to have suffered so much to get to this place. To find myself in a place of no larger purpose, where people die *just because*—this is my nightmare. And to arrive there without warning—without

176

any way to measure how much more time there is before the worst begins, and how long before it will finally be over.

It is my sense that the world is ending, and I can't bear to think it will end amid ignorance and indifference. I want, not just a witness, but a witness who *knows*.

I am doing too many interviews to prepare for. Often more than one each day. I am talking, almost compulsively, about how I don't agree with Bush's rhetoric, about how Americans couldn't possibly approve in the record numbers the polls are suggesting. Is there relief in their eyes?

Is it my imagination, or have they become more emotional? Their faces look different since the terrorist attacks. There seems to be more anger. More threatened tears. More connection to family: mothers lost, children lost, fathers.

Something is breaking open in the *hibakusha*, and everyone needs to know what's inside.

"I walked through the city for days, looking for my aunt first and then for my mother's bones. I remember the blackened streetcar, the electrical wires hanging down, but mostly, there were so many dead bodies. Many women with their heads submerged in water basins—dead—I still remember the long, black hair floating in the water. There were bodies in the rivers, not moving, so many crammed together in layers. Bodies still lying where they died along the streetcar line. You could scarcely pass. There was no clean up yet. No buildings. Everyone was naked; everything was burned.

"The city was so hot. It was all ashes, two or three inches of white and grey ash over everything. I can't remember others searching, or any soldiers, or people cremating bodies. In my mind, it seems quiet. Lonely. My sense is that I was the only one.

"I went back to my house ten days after the bombing. It was completely burned. I found one rice bowl complete and unbroken. It was dark blue. But everything else, the spoons, forks, iron, it was all melted, twisted and stained. There were two piles of ash where my mother and brother had died. The fires had cremated them.

"Their bones were so white in the ashes. They gleamed in the sunshine."

—Seventy-seven-year-old female survivor

CYCLE AND RETURN. The hand back, the pointing finger, to motherhood. My mother stars in every story. *She saved my life. She pulled me out. She screamed for me to leave her before the firestorm surrounded the house.* And when she dies and her child is too young to understand; when the infant can't find the milk at his dead mother's breast: that is heartbreak.

*I cremated her—I was six—I dragged pieces of wood, wooden rail ties, off the bridge and piled them on top of her. I knew that was what she would have wanted. I set it on fire.*

But mothers are also unarticulated. *I'm not sure of her age then. She looked—well, like an ordinary Japanese woman. She wore her hair? . . . like an ordinary Japanese woman. I'm sorry I can't tell you what she looked like. I think she was small.* When you try to sift her pieces out, to pick her apart, bone by bone, she loses form and meaning. She is something felt, not there in the details. She does not exist except in the presence of her children.

MY OWN CHILDREN—how do they remember me? If something were to happen here, what details would they carry in their minds? On black and white paper, echoes of me, frozen in anecdote; an angle of chin fading. With each passing year, I would look more like a stranger, until the woman in the photograph and the mother in the heart were no longer one.

People ask me: *Don't you miss your children?* As if my feeling for them is attached to where I am, declared by a physical place, that I couldn't be here if I loved them. Can't I be? Is "missing" attached to a specific body's presence? How could it be when so many people I have spoken to cannot describe their own mothers?

They ask: *Don't they miss you?*

So far away, I wonder: do they? And if they don't, as they seem not to when I call them, as they seem fine, busy, surrounded, perhaps, by so much love, so many grandparents, aunts, friends, and their father that they have no fear of being alone, what is a mother then? What do we give to our children that remains, long after our hairdos fade? The Maiden I spoke with credited her mother with her life, but could not remember what they talked about. She was convinced of her mother's dedication, yet had very few memories of her.

It is not just descriptive detail that mothers slip away from during my interviews; even in memory, they are unmoored. I know my own mother intimately: I know her blood, the sound and smell of her movement, and yet I am surprised by the fact that she was my age now when I graduated from high school. This fact should be a reminder, yet it drops like a piece of fresh news. She is mine—where I came from, where I have recorded my identity—yet I cannot access most of our lives together. There is no concrete proof that we both were there. When I think of it this way, there is panic. And still she comes to me, now more than ever, in new poses, with words that I can't be sure she ever said. It is a comfort that visits me; it's that sense of comfort that we miss, and mourn.

We don't have to know who our mothers are to love them, but to be a mother, we have to know who our mothers were. When my mother was thirty-six, what did she look like beyond the photographs? What image is uncaptured? What memories are mine?

When I was thirty-six, I took my four-year-old son to pre-kindergarten for the first day of school. And when it was time to go, he turned to me with his small, trembling chin, and said: "Mommy, I will always remember you." Now, in Hiroshima, I am thirty-seven, and a man in his seventies who will not talk about the war or the bombing tells me about his mother:

*I still talk to her everyday, though she's been gone more than thirty years.*

*I miss her so.*

|

## DO YOU THINK ABOUT WAR?

|

AMI AND I ARE looking for beer.

We find it in an outdoor beer garden set up just northeast of Hiroshima Castle; we grab a plastic table and some Kirin in paper cups. It's Sports Day. On this gravel and dirt rim around the moat, in the field of red and white striped

Kirin umbrellas, we have found fair food, and some kind of game Ami can't identify being played beneath a huge balloon—a child's head on the body of a globe. There are children, everywhere; most of them small.

There is a pause—this day is a pause. I have not spoken to Brian in several days, and in this silence, the world is saved. The *taihens* are fading, I am not such a magnet anymore for strangers who swerve off their paths to ask, *America-jin, desuka?*, followed by *it's terrible: taihen*. If I have been ranting, against the rhetoric and fears that are urging retaliation; if I once thought vulnerability would bring empathy—I am still naïve, still very much alone.

*Hiroshima has made a protest to your government . . .*

*. . . a rash act, ignoring the wishes for survival of the human race . . .*

*We vehemently protest . . .*

In Hiroshima, now, there is more fear. In this pause, this beer garden, we have come to test it. Long before September 11, I asked Ami to help me "find the shadow," the emotion that must have been burned into the persons of every Hiroshima citizen, even those who were not yet born. This is my quest—to find the past in this very modern city—and in the wake of the *taihens* and the realization in the eyes around me that America is not as civilized as was once supposed, I have begun to glimpse it. What Ami's interest in all this is, though, I've never been sure.

"Let's talk to people," she says. Her cup is empty. "How about that guy? Are you ready?"

I freeze. *Talk to people?* About what?

"Anything. You pick the questions. I'll translate. What about those two?"

*Wait a minute. A question. A question? Think of one.*

"What about him?"

"I don't know . . . " What don't I know? What more is there to hope for? "Okay. Here's a question. Ah . . . .hmm . . . 'Do you think about war?'"

"*Sumimasen!*" Ami calls to get the attention of two high school-aged boys, and suddenly they are at the table. Rangy, slouching, one of them is wearing a towel on his head folded over as if he escaped from a beauty salon. Their hair is dyed; one is showing a strip of very taut belly above his pants. Both have cell phones.

Very polite.

*Yes, I guess I think about war.*

They are talking about America, and Bush, and what will happen next with the same level of interest as they might have responded to *Do you think about camping?* No mention of World War II. So I ask, "Do you think about World War II and the atomic bombing?"

Not really.

Is there anything in this city, about this city, that makes you think about the bombing?

Well, there is the Gembaku Dome . . . But, not really.

*Domo arigato gozaimashita.*

The next two *sumimasens* yield nothing. An older woman who does not want to talk, a bald man with a lost child in tow who promises to return but doesn't. Then a couple in their fifties walks by.

"Do you think about war?" Ami asks them.

*Yes, oh yes.*

Yesterday, the woman begins, they went to Iwakuni and saw the place where the kamikazes took off during the war. Sixteen-year-old boys who wanted to give their lives to protect their mothers. So she has been thinking a lot about war. These boys are just like the ones in Afghanistan: indoctrinated. They are going to give their lives. She has tears in her eyes. Ami is trying to do a simultaneous translation under her breath, but the woman is focused on me, communicating her concern, her eyes red, and I am trying to communicate back empathy and agreement. The woman is on the proverbial roll—no questions would even be heard—Bush is doing the wrong thing, and Hiroshima should respond; Hiroshima has a responsibility to teach the world what war truly is. She keeps talking about food and water, that they should be the focus, not bombing civilians. She gets into a riff, where food and water chase each other around with not bombing civilians and the kind man standing with her is looking thoughtful and trying to talk, but there is no room. She is leaning toward me, taking off her glasses to wipe her eyes, still talking about food and water, clutched by her conviction that bombing civilians is wrong.

It seems it could be the beginning of something. When the couple is gone, we are giddy. We could do this, from time to time, in a spare moment, Ami says: grab people, ask them questions. I consider this offer as I look at my friend, younger than I am; I have met the parents she lives with, who are not *hibakusha* themselves; I've gone on excursions with her, thanks to her vaguely jobless state. Ami asks for nothing—no money, no favors, no compensation for her tireless translations. It's her pleasure, she says; she is a peace activist. She is doing something good, something that presents itself in the world as needing to be done. But now, as I look into this face I've come to recognize in silhouette and half-light—the beauty mark, the outsized smile—I have to ask:

"Why do you do this? All of this, for me. Why does it matter?"

At ground zero of the world's first atomic bombing, it is peaceful. We sit on the edge of the moat, looking toward the white-winged castle on the opposite bank, framed in an angular skeleton of scaffolding. This was the headquarters of the regional military during the war, now being refurbished, put on view.

"You have been to the Peace Museum," Ami ventures. "What did you see?

"I was in elementary school," she continues. "We went as a class. I was maybe nine? Ten? It was a group of us, silly girls, oohing about anything, making a fuss. We were supposed to answer questions about what we saw, and in the first rooms, so many kids were crowded around the same boxes. I remember I was looking for something interesting . . . "

Then she tells me about Shin's tricycle.

Shinichi Tetsutani was three years old when the atomic bomb was dropped on Hiroshima. He was playing in the yard on his beloved tricycle at that moment, and he died later that day. His father buried Shin's tricycle with him because he couldn't bear to think of his three-year-old boy alone in the ground. Forty years later, when Shin's bones were moved to the family plot, the charred and twisted tricycle was donated to the Peace Museum. And because of this single, rusted exhibit, Ami can no longer step foot into the Peace Museum.

"No one," she says, and her voice is shaking, "should have the power to make another person—*any* other person—bury his three-year-old son."

The sun is setting, catching us in pink and gold; the tips of the trees are flaming; the rising night is calling the stars out; people are gathering their families and going home. In the last drops of the day, an occasional carp floats out of the depths of the water. Orange and white, appearing and disappearing.

What did I see when I went to the Peace Museum? How could I have missed a story like Shin's?

I remember my anger, my impatience. I was looking for proof, for missing pieces, perfectly formed to fit into my puzzle. I wanted answers but I didn't want to answer. And in my anger at my own great capacity to ignore what was in front of me, I managed to blind myself with my own self-absorption. It was the young woman from my book who I wanted and her only: it was her face. If I could restore her identity, if I could see her, then I could finally see beyond her, to history as it was, to my mother, and even to myself.

But what did I *see*?

"Parents who lose a child," Ami says in the quiet, "they have no purpose. That's why I care. There are so many stories about the *hibakusha*—too many to absorb. But there is always one story that will stay with you. Always.

"You just have to find it."

|

## OCTOBER 9, 2001

|

EIGHT A.M. Kimiko calls and wakes me up to say that the war has begun. The United States bombed Afghanistan last night.

"On August 5, my uncle, two aunts, and two cousins came to visit us. They brought rice and vegetables from their hometown in the country. Of course, none of us could have imagined that an atomic bomb would be dropped the next day.

"They were trapped in the house. I remember my two cousins were missing. They had left the house just before I did, headed in the other direction. And we still don't know how or where they died.

"I was only eight hundred meters from the explosion. I was trapped too, and badly burned; my face was swollen and all of my skin peeled off. My mother was also burned. It's all coming back to me now. The glass shards sticking out of my mother's skin. Ahhh . . . I remember.

"We couldn't go home, so we went to my aunt's house, but we were driven away even though we had nowhere else to go to. They called us murderers, and blamed us for my cousins' deaths. They were at our house, so we were responsible. I remember there was some talk that our burns were contagious, that it was an epidemic, which might also have been the reason. They might have been afraid.

"Whatever it was, my mother and I were driven out in the middle of the night."

—Seventy-one-year-old female survivor

# GO-GO BOOTS

MINI SKIRT, waist length hair—who is this woman with the sidelong smile? The parted lips, the secret, hovering?

My mother.

The last time I was in Hawaii, my father charged me with getting rid of the evidence. Too much had accumulated, too much that they would never need. I was put to work: the tosser of mildewed shoes and half-used bottles of foundation. I was also to be the repository of my mother's lost proficiencies: of her cookbooks, now that my father had taken over the meals; the novels she could no longer stick with; clothes she could no longer wear. My mother followed me around, wanting to try on everything, turning the books over in her hands to declare they looked so interesting! On one of those days, when I was going through the cupboards, I found the stacks of old photo albums and put them aside for later. I knew what was in them; I wanted to revisit them alone.

It was not the time to ask my father, even had he been beside me, how old my mother was in this photograph. She seemed so young, but when I did the fashion math it was clear that, unless she was a true visionary and trendsetter, she was already married in these photographs, and more than that, I was already born. This, then, not "my mother before," but my mother.

Who is "mother" separately from the rest of us?

My mother cannot answer. But I can ask her anyway.

It has occurred to me that I am losing my mind, a grown woman dreaming of her mother. In the absence of Brian, or perhaps in our estrangement, or maybe in the nascent presence of my unconscious self, I feel unaccountably fragile—me, the formerly sturdy daughter. There are days when I see my mother in the crowd and imagine she is here, in Japan. I imagine her dead, and that this is where the dead go, that this may be the next place for her as she moves through many lives; this is the place that will make up for all the things she didn't get to do in the life when she belonged to me. I know it's ridiculous, yet, in those moments, I want to chase her, push past the strangers, to speak. But I don't have the words.

Maybe the words would be about the go-go boots. The clicking heels, the extra inches, the center of the world thrown forward with her hips. The life I wasn't aware of as a child, the textures—leather and the feathers woven into the tunic sweater in the photo—that she must have felt against her cheek but can't remember. When would she have worn these? How, in a life that always seemed defined by all she didn't do, could my mother have also been a woman? And what kind? How can it be only now, at age thirty-seven, that I am learning that a mother is also a woman? A female adult, with her own name?

This is my problem, my challenge. And if that sentence keeps recurring, if my personal narrative has become the litany of problems I never knew I had, of assumptions that have constricted my vision so completely I don't even know where opinions end and axioms begin, it is still true, a fact: every minute of my life has been lived within relationship. Defined by relationship. Child for the first half, then wife. This is the beginning of blindness—the ease of that track, the impossibility of wandering off the path—this is how attention begins to atrophy. Before coming to Japan, I never thought of myself as auxiliary, nor did I think of my mother that way . . . but of course I must have felt it because I did not want to be a mother; I did not want to give up the independence I had, at least in my imagination, only to find myself buried so deep beneath the needs of others I could no longer breathe. I must have noticed I was missing definition because I am here, in Japan, following a small group of people who, after having obeyed every rule and requirement of citizenship, found themselves abandoned in the rubble of the end of the world.

And more than just a definition: an instinct, a feeling.

Who was my mother alone? She went from her parents' house to her husband's at the tender age of nineteen, in much the same way I did at seventeen, though with more legal formality. She'd protested that I was too young to live with a boy, *Oh, honey, you have your whole life ahead of you, don't rush into anything. If it is meant to be you will find each other . . . later . . . when you are older.* The fact that Brian could change the light bulbs, "take care of things," these quieted her but did not change her mind. At the time, I was surprised because my mother liked Brian, because she was the one I counted on to approve domesticity, her daughter settled, happy. Now, with this new perspective—perhaps no truer than any other?—she is, differently, but still, surprising. She wanted me to have my youth.

Did she also miss out on her own youth? I wonder now: a woman whose children had all left home by the time she was my age; a woman who was free again at an age when I can still feel in my body what youth is, maybe now more than ever; who had less than two decades of that freedom before she began to lose her mind? Only the girl in the go-go boots can answer that question.

I can ask her now.

"In spring 1945 when the children were evacuated, I was attending Nakajima elementary school, which was called Nakajima National School during the war. I was twelve years old.

"When I parted from my parents and my sister, I was very, very sad. At first, I only thought about what they were doing now in Hiroshima without me, but then, I began thinking about the past. I regretted the fact that I wasn't good to my parents. They always worried about me. I thought, 'When I go home, I will do this or that, all these good things, and I will make them happy.' I always thought I would be going home soon because Japan was winning the war, as we were taught.

"My most vivid memory during the evacuation is hunger and homesickness. I ate almost all edible weeds that I could get. Some kind of locusts and leopard frogs were served on the table. So we were having a very, very hard time. Long before the evacuation, food was already scarce. We couldn't get rice, so substitutes like soybean cake and soybeans were distributed.

"During the evacuation, there was one occasion when our parents were coming to visit us. We children wanted to make them happy, so we got together and talked about how we could do that. It was a very hot season. We soaked and cooled towels in a cold well for our parents and waited. It was just a half-day visit, and it was the last time most of the children would ever see their parents.

"My aunt came to get me on September 15, one month after the war was over. The rest of my family had died."

—Sixty-eight-year-old man

|

# OCTOBER 10, 2001

|

NOON IS TEN P.M. in New York and my oldest son is crying because he misses me.

Noon is Lance Murikawa over coffee at the International House in Tokyo, third interview in eighteen hours, my second of the day, with a tape that does not roll in the first thirty minutes. Noon before, I was on the *shinkansen* where *keitaidenwa* are not allowed. I am living on the other side of time, always inconvenient when I call home; I am speeding through the time I have here, shuffling the top cards that Tokyo has to offer—people, books, resources I can't find in Hiroshima—all of these and the latest bits of news too. Today, I will look at the articles my father has sent on the percentages of Americans who want Arabs to be put into internment camps in the wake of the terrorist attacks, and about the escort system that has been put into place in my own Brooklyn neighborhood by a Japanese American child of the internment to help the Muslim women get back and forth safely to the grocery stores. Tonight, I am giving a lecture.

It's been a month since the attacks and the world is still shifting, uneasy. Brian and I call regularly, but we don't talk. We have no reports to make, no days to share, and it may be my imagination but every time our conversation has run its course from little to nothing, I can feel Brian smirk: the thing he was waiting for did not happen, whatever unnamed "thing" that is, and he takes satisfaction in knowing that I failed once again just as he predicted—in ticking it off the list.

I have not spoken to my boys in days. They don't ask for me. Not until this night strikes New York and Ian is gasping for air amid his tears because he misses me; when he suddenly needs to hear my voice and he is trying to leave a message on my voicemail, trying to say words, make sounds, when my five-year-old son is trying to reach me but I don't hear it—not until the tape is over and lunch is finished, long after he has turned over into restless sleep.

This is what I don't know until it happens: how hard it is to breathe.

Is he sleeping?

WHEN I FIRST FELL IN LOVE with Ian, his eyes were closed. It was two weeks after he was born. I had spent those two weeks recovering from an emergency cesarean surgery, barely able to hold him, existing in a stunned shell that didn't even look like me, a relic who'd survived the gauntlet to the operating room naked, puking and on her knees, who had been overtaken by scalpels and morphine and was now defined by cracked, throbbing nipples, sodden shirts, and a baffling but pervasive despair. When I could finally walk up the stairs on my own, my parents returned home, leaving me and my new family in my hands. And in that moment I remember, Brian had run downstairs to perform the time-honored New York task of moving the parked car from one side of the street to the other. Ian was nursing, and it was suddenly—a new experience—only him and me.

How could I ever forget the quiet in the living room? I felt as if I was floating. Alone with my child, in this unfamiliar, unanchored sense of being—as I watched his small lips purse and pulse at my breast, as I dissolved into the tears of encountering a real, breathing person in my arms for the first time—I could have only one, peculiar thought. They are words that make no sense, and yet they're the ones that come back to me now. Commitment. A promise to guide him through: *Someday, my love, you will be a man.*

BUT NOW, IT IS THREE A.M. and he is not a man. He is a boy who doesn't think about time zones or his parents' struggles, who doesn't count the number of times I've called this week before he decides whether to feel sad. He is asleep at last and I am in Japan—with a useless phone, and an incomprehensibly sad voice message, and the sense of doom that arises from the knowledge that there is more than a small boy who needs me in my house in New York, there is a father enraged. Brian's voice precedes Ian's message, a voice of fists, of trembling. He doesn't know where I am, though I told him on the phone last night when I got to Tokyo. He doesn't think about how I cannot take a call in the middle of an interview; that it is a limitation with consequences, but also one that is real. He wants me to answer. He wants this to be over. This whole thing, this whole life that has happened since June 19, he is waiting for it to be over, for everything to be the way it was before. He wants me to make everything better, and there is nothing I would like to do more. But I am stuck. No matter how many times

I do the arithmetic, I keep getting the same sum: because of the time difference, I will be in the middle of my lecture tonight when they wake up, eat breakfast, and go to school. During the only window when I can reach my children, my cell phone will once again be off.

"The recent terrorist incident. Bush is calling this a new war, a holy war, and he is leveling Afghanistan in the name of that war. What in hell are Americans thinking? Forgive me, but I thought that there are many Christians in America. If they are good Christians, how can they do such terrible things? In the Bible, it says that if someone smites you on your left cheek you are to offer them your right cheek as well . . . Anyway, what America is doing is ten times, a hundred times out of proportion. What is a holy war—more like murder, isn't it?

"If you accept that humans are the highest animal in the animal kingdom, how is it that we are also so unexpectedly stupid? We should work to give our children and grandchildren a legacy—an end to war, and a peaceful world to live in—that is surely the best thing we could leave them. It would be a type of compensation to the three million people who lost their lives in the Pacific War; compensation to the A-bomb victims. It is our duty to bring this into effect."

—Seventy-seven-year-old male survivor

|
# WITHOUT LANGUAGE
|

LIVING WITHOUT LANGUAGE calls the authority of words into question. I've encountered this in my interviews—when the *hibakusha* tell their story, the same one, over and over, their experience becomes the story: they lose the ability to see what was over the hill, what the ruins of the kitchen looked like, if they are never asked. Memory is not history, as I once thought. Memory is narrative, and they are rewriting their lives. Their experiences, which precede words, are reshaped by the words they use for description. If they were stuck once, in their rosy peace narrative, visions of biohazard teams swarming New York offices have expanded their vocabulary now.

I have always believed "things" and their definitions were one and the same. But here, since Japanese often does not translate directly into English, I've discovered that much of what I once would have called "words" are truly "codes." As a writer, I should understand: I've always used these codes to convey a general outline, then brushed in a few details that might not already have been assumed. *Bathroom*, for example, brings up a fairly standard image in America, so I can emphasize the color of the tile, or the soap scum around the sink handles, or the array of partial shampoos on the lip of the tub.

As a person, though, do I know the weight I'm wielding? In Japan, I've given up on words, not wanting them to choose my life and constrict my vision. If I am asked now, could I describe myself? Would I be my description?

Why is it that my strongest sense these days is not of who I am, but what I don't want to be?

I keep encountering the opposite of what I thought I was looking for. When I consider Japan, look at the differences between me and the people around me, I end up confronting my own culture. "Bathroom" is completely non-descriptive in Japan, but it's not the mistranslation that has me tangled. It's the unforeseen labels of my own homogenous culture; the assumptions, even the religion, inherent in certain concepts.

Motherhood, for example.

Why is *mother* the single, most determining splinter of a woman's identity—more than female, Japanese American, college-educated, Hawaii-raised; more than writer, more than daughter, more even than wife? What is this label, and what does it feel like inside this label? What is it to be this code?

There is a narrative we are creating called motherhood. We define it in relation to others—by what mothers do for their children, what our own mothers did for us. It's a rigid story, without permutations or breathing space. It is measured in sacrifice and loss:

*My mother worked two jobs for me* or *she never worked so she could take care of us full-time.*

*She never went on vacation without us.*

*The only night she wasn't actually in the house with us was the time she had to stay over in the hospital.*

*She never left us. Not even for a day.*
*Your husband must be a saint to have let you go.*

I was a mother once. But if I can no longer find myself in this story, am I still?


| |


Dear Reiko-san,

My youngest daughter's name is Reiko, too. Isn't that a coincidence?

Thank you for your letter. My health is not good these days, so I am not sure if I can agree to an interview. However, if I return to Japan while you are still there, I will contact you again.

In this package, I am including some material that might be of interest to you: my book of poetry and some documents on the Tule Lake internment camp.

*Gambatte*. Good luck with your research.

Sincerely,
Lily Onofrio

# |
# RABBITS
# |

IT'S A SMALL, DRY ISLAND covered in bunny rabbits who chase down tourists for their *arare* crackers and will eat out of my hand. A shifting, calico mass meets the ferry, which only Ami and I disembark from, and, as we wander together around the deserted bend to the wide grassy grounds of the government-run hotel where we'll be staying the night, I am reminded of my children on the stage at their school pretending to be "hundreds of cats, thousands of cats, millions and billions and trillions of cats." The rabbits shy up close to the edge of the sandy beaches where Ami and I are sitting on a fence, fully clothed despite the weather. They loiter outside the poison gas museum to wait for us.

Okunojima, the island we are visiting, was taken over by the military during the war and turned into a bustling compound for poison gas production and experiments. Fifty years ago, factories dotted the land, veined with wide pipes, strung with deadly drums and cisterns, pumping who knows what from the plentiful combs of exhaust pipes. Now, if you take one of the creaking mama-san bikes that the hotel rents out on an honor system, you can see what little remains. Bits of bunkers set back into hillsides. An abandoned brick arch. A naked floor.

The small museum consists of one room with the exhibits described only in Japanese. Nondescript bags and rusted canisters and tubing. Gas masks. The photos of tatters and

boils, of human devastation, need no translation. Ami points
to a series of panels that describe brutal experiments:

*How long can a person live if you cut off his legs?*
*What if you gas him at the same time?*
*What if you dip the stumps in poison?*

The poison gas was used in China, but, despite the
hooded, heavily padded protective garments displayed in
both adult and child sizes, many of the casualties were workers and schoolchildren who lived on the island. In the waning days of the war, when desperation was at its height and
the Japanese Navy and the Air Force were out of weapons
and manpower and even sufficient fuel to reach its enemies',
shores, Japan began filling balloons with poison gas to float
them across the Pacific Ocean. Of the nine thousand spheres
they launched, a couple hundred landed in America, caus-
ing a number of small brush fires. Who knows where the
rest landed, what damage they may have caused to the environment, perhaps even to Japan itself? How can anyone be
so bent on destroying the enemy that they can take such terrible risks with their own safety?

I no longer understand what war is. When I was growing up, war was the thing that happened when bad people
were hurting good people and it was our job to stop them.
If it became murkier from there; if the bad guys could be
pretty dastardly, and the good guys quite misguided, there
was still no room for balloons full of poison killing not only
their children, but your own. There were rules, and the aim
was still, nominally, peace.

But what is peace? I no longer understand peace either.

How can the power to blow up two hundred thousand people in one stroke be peace?

It is not death that undoes me, but rampant destruction. It's the cusp of helplessness, the knowledge, too late, that *this is wrong*. It is me, in my imagination, frozen as something terrible unfolds in front of me. Not anything I intended, but exactly what I wrought.

When is *after the bomb*? When will it finally begin? When the world is flat—a desert of sand where once two of the greatest skyscrapers stood—when there is no longer even a window to look out onto the black world of ash, how long will we continue to think, "this can't be real"?

For how many days, or months, or years, will we wake up unprepared, expecting to see the old world, the one we wanted, the one that we thought we had the right to in those far away days when we were innocent?

"I remember seeing the soldiers off at Yano station. The Rising Sun flag flying, we elementary school students singing our army songs with a fighting spirit, with cries of 'Banzai, Banzai!' Parting was so difficult—I didn't want to be there. I was crying in my heart, but my face was smiling. And then, at some point, the soldiers would come back, in white boxes containing their bones, or sometimes not even their bones, just a single sheet of paper.

"The unspeakably triumphant return.

"We were taught to have faith. To be loyal. That Japan's war was justice. But to speak simply, we were taught to throw our lives away for the emperor. We didn't know anything about the atrocities that the Japanese soldiers were committing in Asia, instead we were told that the 'Wind of God,' the kamikaze, was on our side. We were thoroughly indoctrinated.

"It's happening now, in Afghanistan. In the midst of America's war on terrorism, there are Islamic children, they go to religious schools and their education tells them to throw their lives away. It's exactly the same. They don't know the truth. But they sacrifice themselves, and they suffer—the women and children suffer the most. In a long war, goods become scarce. Food becomes scarce. And then the husband is taken, the father is taken, and killed. The victims of those bombings, errant bombings, they are just struggling to survive."

—Sixty-five-year-old male survivor

## |
## JANE IS WAITING
## |

MIDDAY HIROSHIMA. Me on my bicycle. I am navigating the sidewalk on my way to lunch with Jane, weaving behind old ladies, tourists, office girls chatting on their cell phones, teenagers chatting on their cell phones, business men chatting on their cell phones . . . We should all simply implant our phones in our ears—it would cut down on the swerving as the women in long skirts connect long distance while riding their mama-san bikes in high heels. Once I saw a woman on a bike holding a cell phone to her ear in one hand and an umbrella in the other. The umbrella-holding hand was the one resting on the handle bar.

My cell phone rings.

I am late. I am always late when I come to see Jane because she gives me an arrival window, and I always shoot for the last few minutes of that window, even though I know she's probably ready fifteen minutes before I could possibly appear. I wouldn't answer this call, except it has to be Brian, and I missed his call last night for the second time this month. I have excuses—I didn't get home when I expected to and the time difference is difficult; our telephone plan only allows me to call him at home, not at work, and he'd left by the time I could have reached him—each excuse is real even if, together, they are overabundant. I am hurried, in a hurry; still, I imagine that five minutes now and a date for later is better than nothing. I begin with an apology, as

I dismount my bike to talk, my eyes on the corner ahead where I have to turn. I have no time now, but he should tell me what his schedule is so we can set a time to have a good long conversation . . .

Some time in the future. When it's convenient.

There's a noise on the phone that is not a word.

Brian feels abandoned. Again, still, daily, every moment. He is angry, and insists Jane can wait though he has nothing specific to say. Nothing to report, nothing pressing except that I never answer when he calls—

*We have $250 phone bills each month.*

He can never reach me—

*We have sent eighty-three emails in the last ten weeks.*

Where was I back in July when the boys were puking all night in the hall?

*In Japan.*

I've voiced none of these responses. I am simply listening. Or maybe, in truth, I am not listening. Maybe I'm waiting for the sound to end. The voice that's getting lower, sarcastic, unreasonable; that's now accusing me of not caring about my children; that's telling me about a story he read or heard on the radio, something about a father who only gives his kids five minutes a day. I am silent—this is what I do when I feel threatened—and I know that will backfire too. Brian hates it when I shut down like this. Years ago, before we were married, he broke his hand in several places one night because I started cooking dinner in the middle of a fight. I am separating, splintering. I cannot engage in this, so I try to escape. My silence is the reason his voice is changing; I know it on some level, but I've arrived at Jane's office now—she has seen me, has risen; I have signaled through the glass-fronted window of the lobby to please give me another minute. I am caught in her full view as the lunch hour ticks on, with a phone to my ear, and a husband on the other end who has clearly moved from the cautious omission we were practicing so well together into direct accusation. From hoping that I will offer to come home to condemning me for staying.

I didn't expect this. It's not so much that I couldn't have guessed at this underworld, but I never thought it would rise up with such sudden violence.

I was counting on it *not* to rise.

*Please, Brian, please. I'm sorry, but this isn't the right time. I can't . . . We need to talk about this later . . .* I'm getting frantic under Jane's gaze, so these words come out. Unbeknownst to me, she's invited a colleague to join us, and now both women are waiting on the sofa on the other side of the glass. But my pleas make him angrier, and he insists he wants to set his dates to come to Japan. He wants to know when, and how long, and he must decide this minute, at two in his morning.

*It depends . . .* I begin.

There is a second explosion on the other end of the phone. What Brian hates most is when things "depend."

Look at the writer on the sidewalk—for that is what I am now, clearly no longer a mother or a wife—she is almost in tears. She is flaunting personal strife in the street, of all places, publicly inconveniencing one of her benefactors (a chaos she can feel even in the bend of her elbows though it would mean nothing at all to Brian); she is completely unable to comprehend the man she's spent all her adult life with. His words enter her ears—he wants to come to Japan for eight weeks—she can hear the anger, the challenge, the test. She cannot hear his pain. She knows, but cannot feel, what his life is like, and she clings to avoidance, to his now-expired statements that everything is fine. Her expectation that he would support her journey—that he agreed—is long-dead, but she won't concede that. He talks often about how he "gave" her this opportunity, but there is no gift in this anger.

There is my world, and his world, and although both are duly described, neither can conjure the other. He is running a business, raising two kids in a city that's been attacked, and he doesn't have the time to look at the long emails I send about my adventures. It turns out he knows nothing about my trips to Tokyo or any of the main events of the last three months; the last thing he read was a brief description of the fisherman outside my window. He knows nothing of what the writer writes, of how I am recreating my life and why, only that I must be creating something because I am never available. And strangely, incomprehensibly, he has decided that he hates Japan, the place I have pinned my life on.

He hates it.

And me? I have lost the world I lived in; my ability to see him. I have lost my sense of myself, even my understanding of what I'm saying. I am telling him the eight weeks he's proposing is a long time. Japan is expensive; there's no child-care and I know he doesn't want to be a househusband. I get around by bicycle, and in Japan, people don't take their spouses and children out with them to work or social functions. If he wants to live here, make a life for himself, if there is something he wants to study or explore, then he can come now and be welcome. But he has no particular interests in Japan; he has not had any time to think about it because he has no time, period. No time to think, no time to breathe . . .

We could be speaking in a foreign language for how far off the truth our statements are.

I say: *Of course I want you to come. Whenever and wherever; when you are ready; for however long you want.*

I can't hear myself, except from a distance. I can't see myself—how can I tell my own story, be my own narrator, how can I live my own life if I can't hear my lack of attention the way he can, my desperation to escape? Panic—is it panic?—has set in; it has risen, fallen, swelled like the ocean, dropped like darkness, like a net from the sky. It tightens around me, and I am talking now, in circles and loops, compulsive in his silence. I am relying on logic, have blocked out all feeling, and yet I am backtracking, protecting, because there's a breaking point here; this is no simple fight. I am giving in—perhaps this is guilt, then?—because I'm suddenly sure he will not.

And yet, and still, protection has to reach into the future. I make one last pitch against my losses: if he wants to travel, to sightsee as a family, then three weeks might be better. I'm telling him how expensive things are, how traveling as a family means four times the price of one. I don't even know what's possible: I've barely left Hiroshima, except under someone's auspices; have never asked for a hotel room, never tried to rent a car. This is the truth, and reasonable—precisely, exactly—but we are beyond mutual definitions, and these are not reasons he can hear.

And the greater truth is, I don't want to lose the last third of my fellowship. I don't want to be forced to re-make the choice, minute to minute, between my work and my family. It seems I must already make that choice daily, that I've been fighting an unnamed, unlocateable "it" that believes I should not be here, and now, as it locates inside Brian, I wonder whether it has always been there or whether it has just possessed him. I want my husband back, the man who loves me, not the man who swallowed him, the one on the telephone. I don't know how to reach him. I don't know how to assure him I'm still there.

He tells me how. That, even in the face of his fury, I can measure my love for him in days.

He wants a yes or a no, and he wants it now. And so I am caught, making a decision I don't want to make, not this way, in all this swirling resentment, with all the possible dangers I'm trying to convey, but he's no longer listening and not even I can shift through all my excuses anymore.

JANE IS STANDING. It has been more than thirty minutes and I must get off the phone.

Pick a date, Brian is saying. Just pick one. Any date.

This reunion has all the markings of a disaster, but cutting his time short would be even worse. *Your dates are fine*, I tell him. *Your dates are great. November 16 to January 14.*

"We were living in Canada. We got no news, except that the atomic bomb had been dropped on Hiroshima, and then we got a telegram from my grandfather saying, 'Come home, just the four of you.' Meaning, just leave everything and come.

"I was fourteen. I had never been to Japan, and I didn't know the Hiroshima dialect then. I couldn't understand my grandmother and grandfather. Oh, it was terrible when we finally got back—it was fourteen or fifteen days on the freighter and then we got on the train and it was so crowded that you couldn't go to the toilet. Men would jump out of the windows at the stations, but the women, you know, we had to kind of walk on people . . .

"When we got to the station, my grandparents were there, my aunt was there, and all my relatives, and we were so tired but we still had to walk two and a half hours to get home. It was on the mountain, and it was dark, and they kept telling us, 'Keep to the left, keep to the left,' because the other side was a cliff. We had lanterns, but we couldn't see anything. I was in a daze."

—Seventy-year-old Canadian Japanese woman

# UNDERGROUND

THOSE WERE THE DAYS when I was invisible.

My mother sits beside me on the subway train. It's New York City, I am just out of college, in the days when the soles of my shoes still stuck to the dried soda on the vinyl flooring and the graffiti-stained windows would have shone like a church if they were not underground. In memory, the car is almost empty. We have our long, grey bench to ourselves; no one stands between me and the pole in front of me that I will swing past when I explode, flinging my body onto the opposite bench to glare across the way at my mother.

Those were the days I can't remember, unless I try, and then only in shards. In shatters—not a word or at least not the right one, but it's the one that comes to me now and how I felt then. Who knows what was wrong, where this frustration and anger came from? I can't remember if I was still in therapy then—as a teenager I had the disconcerting ability to cut people dead if ever they hurt me, at least beyond the trivial, and I spent some fruitless time discussing that with a college-subsidized shrink. In instances of betrayal, I cut off my own heart for safety. And if it was a pulsing, poisonous safety—heat and nausea that washed through me every time I saw the person—at least I'd found a way to identify the enemy and remove myself from further risk; a solution for which therapy had no such guaranteed alternative.

But perhaps that period in my life was not this time.

I was not married yet. I must still have been starting the career that would go nowhere, of catering to people who wanted to be famous, and who either believed they were not because I was bad at my job, or that my success in garnering attention for them was not really mine but the natural consequence of their wit, their magnetic personalities. In my mother's presence—and why ask where we were going, where we were coming from, why "the guys" weren't there?—I was suddenly struck by the feeling that no one really knew me. What was inside did not fit the outside, and I wasn't sure where the outside came from or what the inside was. Just as now, it was unclear: I had no alternate identity or unacknowledged talent to claim. But I had rage. The wrong persona had been ascribed to me, and I accused my mother, flung it at her that she didn't even know who I was.

I was afraid. Afraid of not recognizing myself, suspicious that the split I felt in my persona was proof that my true self was unacceptable. Worse: unlovable.

It was not just those dreams I had that I was registered for a class I didn't know about, whose final exam I now had to take—in those dreams I always had a day when I might still try to learn everything in the textbook, there was a gauntlet to run, an interlude in which I could try to change the future, even knowing the future was unchangeable, that I would fail. I was not just a perfectionist, not just an overachiever with deep insecurities—in those dreams I was face to face with a world that was not what I was led to believe it was. I was bewildered, inadequate, but still somehow preoccupied with control, tormented by the possibility that I might still be saved, salvaged, that this class could be passed and then swept under the rug, and I wouldn't have to be other than I was.

There was no reconsideration in my dreams. No way to drop the course, change the major, to open oneself to an alternative universe and trust in the future.

My mother said, that day on the train, underground, that of course she knew me. Calmly, as if—*you are my child*. It was both impossible in its assumption and deeply scary. She offered to prove it. What if she was wrong and I was truly invisible in the world?

What if she was right?

There were things my mother said. I don't remember the words. I can see it happening, but I cannot hear. I have lost my mother's declaration of love; her words vanished, no one to say them, no one to remember, as if it never happened, but I cannot allow that. There were things my mother said; these must survive. These things were true, more real than any thought I've ever had about myself, and I need them now. I need to hear my mother's voice, the mother who loved me—*you are my child*—and if I cannot, just now, remember her words, still, the feeling of being unearthed, the strike of the shovel and the slow release of pressure from the soil on my head, these I will never forget.

"I was eight, and I was outside my house when the bomb exploded. There was a bluish flash, and I was blown off my feet, and then it was dark, and there was a strong wind, and the roof tiles, everything fell down on me. I couldn't find my father, and the fires began, and, well, I decided to run away.

"That's when the black rain started. And there was nowhere to hide from it, and no one knew what to do.

"There were so many people lying in the streets, burned and bleeding. The next day I went to the shrine near my house because I wanted to see the city. The stone steps of the shrine were covered with the dead and dying. They pulled on my legs, saying 'help me, help me,' saying it desperately, begging me for water and I was so scared that I couldn't move because their eyes were popping out, and they looked so hideous. There was no way to treat them, but I gave some of them water.

"And then they died. I will never forget that. They drank the water, and I was so happy, I thought I was being good, that the water was cold and good. And then, there were several men and women, I could see their agony; they fainted and stopped moving and all the life ran out of them. I didn't touch them but I could see. And I thought: I killed this person, and I have to keep it a secret. Later that day, my father warned me not to give any of the victims water and I felt so guilty. I felt guilty for years.

"I never told him what I did. I never talked about it either, not for forty-five years, until he passed away."

—Kimiko Uchida

# TRIP TO THE SUBURBS

I AM STANDING in the dark, in the cold, trying to see some trace of where the old kitchen might have been behind this pre-war house that has no electricity. This is the coldest part of Hiroshima prefecture, where the ski resorts have begun making snow for the winter on this late October day, and I am increasingly underdressed in my fleece pullover. Just before all the light left the sky, I was being shown an old, rusted *furo*—an iron tub I could barely have crouched in. Then, a heavy container for water, and then the night was pitch black—no moon or stars; all the houses were lightless since it was 6:30 p.m. on a Sunday night in the country. Minatoya-san, the woman who brought us here, is still valiantly trying to explain what this house she grew up in looked like, but I can't see anything and Kimiko, who stayed up all last night telling me her story and has been translating nonstop all day, is no longer making sense—though it could be me who can no longer hear. This day has been long in the making, Kimiko has been mulling and rejecting towns to find the perfect suburb for me, a country village to set part of my novel in, and Minatoya-san has given the gaijin at least seven hours of her time so far. For my part, I got into the back seat of the car and promptly fell asleep because, on the winding mountain road with no food in my stomach, the alternative was to be sick.

Since my last conservation with Brian, I have been saying *yes* to every opportunity that presents itself, even if it means dinner at eleven p.m. and writing in the few, fading minutes before sleep. I'm surprised to realize I've been doing so for quite a while. I've reached a point where I am gathering, collecting life without requiring it to be relevant. I am doing what Ami's friend talked about—*ichi go* something—engaging in each moment. Before, I was doing it in leisure, turning a tea cup in my hands time and again and slowly, not to catalog every detail and therefore own it, but to acknowledge its existence. Now, though, with the premature finale of my life in Japan looming, I'm getting greedy.

Should I give up my insistence that I will continue my interviews and research once my family arrives? Am I wrong to stand up for myself in my arguments with Brian, especially when I don't know exactly what I'm standing for? Before I came to Japan, this stubborn gut feeling was rare; it was so easy for me to get "talked out" of something. It wasn't that I was forced; I accommodated the most peaceful solution. But now that I can feel my gut, now that it's awake and fighting for the needs I can still meet, I'm surprised at how unyielding Brian's opposition is.

We are in Kaki, and before that, in Geihoku, in Yawata, but I have no orientation, and no idea where those places are. Earlier today, I visited a large traditional farmhouse with a thatched roof made of pampa grass rising easily thirty or forty feet high. The entire exterior was composed of sliding doors—paper screens and stucco—so that in the summer, the farmhouse was completely open to the outside. It was designed, in this very cold weather, to let the hot summer air rise out of the living space and the breeze circulate. The interior was a single, enormous room, with tracks and sliding doors in various places so that each area could be opened or closed and its shape shifted like a puzzle.

The farmhouse was a tourist attraction, and the guides were several very old, bent, and tiny women who were also selling produce and farm products outside. After conferring briefly with Kimiko, they invited us in and began telling stories about their lives in the "old days." We sat around the *irori*, a rectangular hearth cut out of the tatami floor with a small wood-burning fire, and a hook hanging over it for an iron tea kettle or pot, where one of them grilled *mochi* for their guests. They led a brief tour, showed off the interior barn where animals were kept so they didn't freeze to death in the winter. It had been turned into a storeroom, for baskets and buckets and sieves; for the farming equipment: arching two-handled saws, cone-shaped sun hats and raincoats made of untamed straw. They showed off the kitchen, and the two white-stone ovens just for cooking rice. In the old days of these women's lives, it was a woman's job to start the fire and make rice and get the house ready before everyone got up. I was reminded of one of my very modern peace activist friends who, in the year 2001, still rises every morning a half an hour before her husband wakes up "so he can feel like the house is not sleeping." This youngish wife makes no elaborate breakfast—the rice is warm, the miso soup simple—so it's not as if she needs all that time for preparation. It is his comfort, and his request, and after he's gone to work, she goes back to sleep for an hour until her work day begins.

The women talked about the war, and how people made their way back from the bombed city. How many hours it took to walk—uphill, downhill—if you ever wanted to leave. I watched them speak. I looked at their missing teeth, at their faces so gnarled they looked as though beauty had never touched them. Not that they weren't beautiful in their waning years, in their baggy *monpe* clothing and their indigo-dyed head wraps; not that they weren't beautiful when they were young. But they looked as if they'd lived a life in which there was no use for a bit of powder on their cheeks, a kimono with a gay pattern and a flattering color instead of one that was chosen for the warmth. What was it like to live a life without artifice? Where your sole measure was what your body could endure, how many hours of work you could complete, whether you could pull a plow when you had no animal to do it? Not by what you said you were, or could do, but by what you produced.

My life, right now, is the opposite. I'm allowing my interviews to go anywhere, logic and factual details be damned. My days alternate between life and death: between solitude, and hiding from Brian and America, and experience—loving every circle of my bicycle's wheel as I ride along the river, every trip, every person. I have dropped out of my own "old days" before Japan; I am avoiding the constraints and expectations that have become far too visible by refusing to see them, in much the same stubborn way as a young child believes that a person ceases to exist when he leaves the room. I have been put on notice, and every moment is a moment stolen, a different kind of cheating—the cheating of staying in Japan, and standing strong, but not of actually doing the work. I have not begun my new novel; my interviews are not even transcribed. My writing has been narcissistic: reams of paper on what I did that day, but no manuscript to show for it. I've been unable to produce what I came to write.

Unable to face what I truly fear.

It is not my fellowship I'm afraid of losing. It's my life. Every time I forget a word, I think, *so this is how it begins*. I can tell myself I am trying to function in two languages now. I can recall my father's assurances that writers access words at the much slower pace of their fingers; I can treasure the slips of others who comment carelessly that their minds are sieves and they must be getting old. Then, too, pregnancy can rob you of your memory; more than once when I was pregnant I walked into a room and forgot what I went there for. But wouldn't I get that back? Not every woman who has given birth suddenly forgets the word for "television." Even if I don't own one, isn't that a bad sign? And how will I know if there really is a problem, if this thing that is stealing my mother is also in my body and I, too, have only two decades left?

I am my mother's daughter after all. People used to say we could be sisters.

Time is the question. How will I know when time is short, where time should be spent, what to focus on? What of my *own* time: who should I give it to? I know what the answer should be, but still, I want it for myself. Everything I've given my family, so far, seems to have disappeared in one way or another. If this is all I have, all I will ever be, I cannot bear to let it go to waste.

But on my own, I'm not doing much better. I am eating bits of burned, hard *mochi*, and trying not to yawn. Kimiko is the one asking the questions. Kimiko is the one taking the pictures. Kimiko can sense the changes in me, my losses; she knows what I need for the novel, and I trust her absolutely. I need her absolutely. I have no way to guess whether I am hiding or emerging, whether I am healing or being reckless; I can't tell what she understands, or how she will do it, but with the foreign language blurring in my ears, I know Kimiko is the one who will rescue me.

I need to be saved.

"My grandfather was the second son. He was very short, like a monkey, but he was funny, optimistic . . . I liked him very much. He went to Hawaii to work on the plantations in 1895, and he married a woman from Hiroshima while he was there. It was a hard life. He was indentured for at least nine years. My grandparents had three children: my father, his younger brother, and a girl who died.

"After the girl died, my grandmother brought the boys back to Japan to live with her in-laws. The life on those plantations was really appalling—I would have left too, but I don't think it was acceptable in those days. My grandparents eventually got divorced and my grandfather remarried: that was all I knew.

"But then one day, shortly before my father died, we were driving and he pointed to a corner on the street and said: 'That's where I said goodbye to my mother.' The story is that, when he was five, his mother left her in-laws house forever, taking his two-year-old brother with her. He walked with her to that corner, which was quite a way from the house, and then went 'home,' crying all the way. I don't know why she left. Maybe they kicked her out because she abandoned their son in Hawaii. But my father only saw his mother one more time in his life. It was on the day that she brought his younger brother back and left him too."

—Jane Osada

THERE IS ONE SMALL TOWEL, one bit of white terry cloth. In length, if you are using body parts to measure, it should extend from the middle of an average Japanese woman's breasts—just above the nipple—to just beneath her pubic hair. But of course, this is the essential bit of information I am lacking, which Kimiko holds, but doesn't, in her amusement and our privacy, bother to offer. I know that, due to a curious sense of economy, this is the instrument I am supposed to cover with soap and water and use to scrub myself off before getting into the *onsen* water, and it's the same instrument that will dry me off when I am done. There is a bucket too, that serves both as a stool (to sit on while washing) and a container for the wet towel.

I HAVE BECOME Kimiko's daughter, and her friend. She is the one who calls to find out how my day was, even after midnight because she can see my bedroom lights through her window across the river and knows if I'm awake. I am alone, she is alone, and though I didn't ask her to, I appreciate the chat, late at night, the checking in, not much to say. Today, her latest gift to me, she is treating me to a day of lounging at a fancy spa on the tip of Shikoku. The family is coming soon, she says. She does not have to say the words, *You need this*. Between baths, we sprawl together on the comfy sofas in the lobby and nap.

THIS IS THE FIRST TIME I have been privy to the lives of older women. In interviews, sad stories; in my friendships. Here, women who have lost husbands or left them; left children or had them leave or fought to get them back; who have struggled with life and come out the other side. Not monsters, just people. And successful in their own way: loved, forgiven, triumphant, with some regrets but no fatal blow. They look at me, the American taking a hiatus to chase her dream, and they give me what I need: their stories, unspun. I can only guess at the courage it must take to share their lives. And if their stories seem to circle in on their difficulties and choices about mothering, I have no need for their perfection, just as they seem to have no need for mine.

IT WAS JUST YESTERDAY when Jane, too, took me out to "celebrate" at a restaurant that specialized in Okinawan food. "You'll be okay," she said, her face in profile. "My children survived. I told you—I was working a lot. I was traveling, for years I traveled . . . "

Was it the unspoken Jane wanted me to hear in the long pause that followed, or my own narrative? What was it she told me: *my children stayed with my parents . . .*

"It worked out okay."

If Jane and I had barely spoken of her family, I'd said even less about my own. She watched me once, through a wall of glass, fighting with Brian, but that can be all she knows.

"Did I tell you?" she asked then, "I was thinking the other day, about my grandmother." And then she told me her father's memory of the last time he saw his mother as a child. If our conversation seemed scattered, it was exactly on point: how do we know if we can be salvaged, and what will or will not survive? There are no guarantees, only explanations; only choices that must be made and never unmade. I knew what Jane was offering: a model for getting older. She was stepping in for my own mother, to show me how to suffer and survive.

THERE IS ONE BASIC POOL inside the women's *onsen*, and a heavy pour from a pipe that can be used to massage the shoulders. There is a shallow bed of water where four people can lie side by side with their necks resting on wooden pillows and sleep in the water. There is also an outdoor bath built from stones in the courtyard, and this is where I walk, naked among the shrubs where the breeze can lift the heat off my skin. Kimiko lets me go, lets me savor the day without comment. These are my final hours, and we both know it. On our way home, Kimiko will tell me about the modesty of the towel, but until then the tensile casing between me and the world, between me and myself, falls away and there are no rules for behavior. I am naked in Shikoku with a woman who accepts me exactly for whatever I am trying to be.

SHE: "I had yellow blisters all over my body. It hurt so badly. My neck arms and legs . . . There was a first aid station set up at the junior high school, in the auditorium. We were lying on the floor. There was a high school girl next to me. She would cry and roll around and ram into me, which really hurt. Sometimes my husband would lie down between us so she couldn't bump into me."

HE: "They put two tables together—that's where they used to treat people. There was a big man, around forty years old, with severe burns from his neck to his bottom. They used a knife to scrape the burns clean since they had no medicine. There was no anesthesia, and the man was in great pain. It took five or six soldiers to hold him down."

SHE: "Then it was my turn. I didn't want to be treated, even if it meant death."

HE: "But I forced her onto the table. I worried that she might bite her tongue because of the pain, so I stuffed a towel in her mouth."

SHE: "I was there for twenty days, and they scraped me every day. In the beginning, the pus and blood would ooze out like chocolate. It hurt so much, and it would continue to hurt for, oh, eight hours, until the pus formed again. I will never forget it. But it healed little by little from the outer edges. After about ten days, a thin skin formed over my burns and the pus no longer oozed out. So then I became able to endure the pain."

—Married couple, mid-seventies, survivors

A COATLESS MID-NOVEMBER afternoon. Blue sky. On Miya-jima—a small island in the Inland Sea that has been dubbed one of the three most beautiful places in all of Japan—the maples are starting to turn. It is a steep, densely forested place, more like a mountain, or two, rising out of the sea, its clusters of ancient buildings nestled along the shore. Today, fall is looming: bits of ruby, burnt orange, lemon-green scattered among the evergreens. The brilliance is still days away; it won't explode until my family arrives.

I should be home, getting all my loose ends xeroxed, tallied and scrubbed clean, but instead, I am firewalking.

Behind me, the famous torii, huge and vermillion, floating more than one hundred yards offshore, the gate to the entire, sacred island. The tourist arcade of *momiji manju* and wooden rice paddles; the Heian-era Itsukushima Shrine; ornate pagodas; ancient timber halls. At the base of the stairs to Daisho-in, the Buddhist temple, on the first of hundreds of wide granite slabs, I'd put my hand out to brush the running golden handrail, to roll my fingers over each of the vertical spinning cylinders within it, each inscribed with kanji; they are a chant, more than one, and spinning them is the spiritual equivalent of prayer. I'd passed between the squat bald *jizos* sitting on either side of each stair, each gazing toward his balancing partner through my running feet. I am making the most of my last days of freedom, partaking in a ritual that has captivated me ever since I first heard of it.

Walking through fire.

In front of me, then: a wide clearing of dirt amid a quadrangle of temple buildings. It's hard to see through the heads, six or seven deep, of Japanese tourists, but there is an altar on one end of the clearing, and in the center, a square pyre, stacked like open lattice Lincoln logs and stuffed with pine needles. There are eight monks preparing for the ceremony, robed in gold and white and heavily beaded; thick, black plastic cups strapped onto their foreheads on their closely shaven heads. Partially, intermittently, I can see they are arranging wishes on the end furthest from the altar.

One thousand yen for a wish, and I have made one. On this crisp, unscheduled day, I dropped my money in a box, accepted a bit of pine plank and a Sharpie, and wrote down my name, birth year, address, and my wish. If it's meant to be, I'm told, it will come true. Thousands of planks have been filled out and are waiting in the boxes. I don't know what they're waiting for; I don't know what is meant to be, or appropriate to ask for, but I know what I want. I want to experience the world around me fully, without blocking, or organizing, or rehearsing my way on a map. I don't want to be capable, or well-defined.

I want to feel.

My latest leap of faith taken—that Buddha can read English—I hand in my wish just as several men appear on the *engawa* that wraps the main temple and climb up onto the saddle of a large taiko drum. One drummer stands before the face, shouting, using his entire body to whip a baton against it. The blows get caught in the cleft of the hills and sharpen around us as the echoes of each are exactly superimposed. As I tiptoe to see, a few of the older people around me begin chanting softly.

In the space, the monks have begun to purify each corner, first with fistfuls of rock salt that spray into my hair, then with water, then with wands of white paper chains, the kind I have seen visitors shake over each others' shoulders when they enter the shrine. The monks are also chanting, but the ritual is oddly casual: in the highly stylized world of Japan, they act more like fast-food workers in America—muttering, gesturing, checking stock, moving boxes—as they complete their assigned tasks. The ceremony coheres bit by bit: by the time the paper wands come out, the chant is rapid and organized; once the monks grab their weapons, their movements are composed. I am no devotee of religious ceremonies, but this is my first opportunity to watch black-cupped human unicorns wield swords, or chop heart shapes into the air with cookie-cutter axes, or pull back a bow and shoot arrows into the crowd. The arrows arc in all the corners except mine, where one flies straight up and then straight down directly over our heads, leaving me to duck to avoid the lunging old people who are trying to catch it for luck. There is a brief mêlée, which ends with a stunned, grey-haired gentleman lying on the ground. I watch his body bounce, watch him get his senses and then his bearings, before he dusts himself off and joins the chant again.

Two of the monks have picked up small broom-like torches and lit them on the flames on either side of the altar; my gaze leaves the man in time to see them plunged into the pyre. Smoke stirs softly: a puff, but very quickly it begins to boil with the same wild power I have seen rising off the ocean when lava hits the shoreline. It is a living creature in the center, stretching into screens and strands as it awakens. When the wind grabs it, the contour scatters and spreads, but the center continues to churn, animated, like the cumulus clouds in Hiroshima's summer sky. Which means, not only does it have urgency, it also has edges, and shadows, and light.

It's over me, and I feel blessed. It's high enough that I have no trouble breathing—I can feel the heat and watch the smoke dissolve, like sea spray, into droplets. There are, like there is in the summer sky, too many formations. But these surround me; they swallow me, I expect them to fall on my skin like rain.

*My mother is standing in the darkened hallway, the light from her bedroom room illuminating part of her face.* Her eyes are still bright. If I hadn't worked so hard to shut down my own terror, we might have created a different memory. This is what I want now. The courage to reach out to hold her. To linger, even in the pain, if it means getting my mother back.

The fire has become a furnace, blazing thirty feet into the air, rippling the monks out of shape. People are coughing; eyes are stinging; the chant is growing with the sheets of blowing flame. Each monk has a box—more than one—of our wishes. And their job, at the four corner stations, is to glance at each wish and then to throw them in bunches into the fire.

Eight monks. Forty-five minutes. Ten dollar wishes flung in fistfuls into the pyre so they will burn, cool, turn to ash. This is what we will walk on: our hopes, private needs, and impossible fantasies, all of them absorbed through the soles of our feet. Every image is vivid, every person, every smell. My wish is in the smoke, and on the path before me: I am more porous. I am standing in line, inching closer as the pilgrims in front of me step forward in twos, bits of each of us clinging to them, to the others, our hopes for the future working their ways into someone else's heart.

Into our own.

"We were waiting for my sister to return. Moto. She was sixteen. They had conscripted her to work in the munitions factory, so she was on Misasa Bridge when the bomb was dropped. She was terribly burned.

"I really, really hate this. This part is the most difficult. But it is also the truth. At the time, there were air raid warnings frequently. When the sirens were blaring, there was a blackout regulation, so we covered our light bulbs with umbrellas, and then a dark cloth so that just a spot shone on the floor. The night after the bombing, all of the lights were off, so inside and outside it was really dark. My mother sat on the veranda all night, waiting. She wouldn't come in.

"The next day, a man came to tell us where Moto was, and they brought her home, lying on a door. Her clothes were tattered and stuck to her skin. She died the next night, calling, 'Mother, help me, please.' And that condition, my sister's agony, her terrible burns, her skin slithering off . . . that scene, that terrible scene, it was common at the time. If I try to talk about it, to put it another way, the flash and the absolutely terrible . . . to try to convey it in a single word, our experience of the war as children, it was a poor . . . hard . . . scary . . . life.

"A very painful, frightening life."

—Seventy-year-old male survivor

# A LACK OF WORDS

I FOUND IT AT LAST. The shadow.

It's in his tears, his insistence on running through his story—not for me, not in answer to my questions—but for himself. He starts where he wants to, and finishes in the same place. He lost his sister in the bombing, and he still has her clothes.

He paints the *pikadon* in watercolors every day.

Here is a man who was eaten by anger. His speeches so full of rage that Ami spent three months searching for a go-between to ask if he would talk to us. He has traveled the world, scolding and condemning. I wanted to feel this, to hear what he has to say.

But my role today is not to interview. It is to sit while he relives it, while he tries to make sense of it, while he releases the pressure that will rebuild in him too soon. With his first words, I realize he has let go of the anger he was famous for. And now, in his outpouring, there is no space between him and his story. No wall to protect him from his anguish—only terrible healing.

His sister's face is as clear for him as it was that day; her cries; his mother's grief, his mother's refusal to leave the veranda, to give up, to allow that the war might have taken her child. He brings them with him, to this rented room in a community center where he must sit in a chair because of his pain. He is feeling ill, he always feels ill, this day is worse than others but not as bad as some, yet he insists he will speak; he has even brought a folder with pages of proof. Of life before the bombing, and after, of his family as they existed in his mind. He has his *pikadon*s, and he wants me to have one.

He is ready.

And for an hour, his sister Moto will come home. His mother will smile, his friends rise from the dirt, the skies will not tremble. He will get on the train to deliver the miso paste to his oldest sister instead of being knocked to the ground. He will not see the *pikadon*, a grain of rice, tinged with yellow and growing, or the fireball he has put in my hands: red as blood, speckled orange, small as a flame, a blossoming flower, with the heart of an angry rainbow, edged in black as it grows. For an hour—if he allows himself to feel it—joy will come back with the sorrow, and his wishes too; he can have his own heart back, beating with the knowledge that someone else *knows*.

They did not die in vain. They did not disappear. Another person sees, and maybe that will make a difference.

He needs me as much as I need him. He builds his safety one person at a time. One image at a time. Each painting, each new mushroom cloud, a new instant and still too many to purge. Both in anger and in sorrow, he is trying to make witnesses, witnesses who have never seen that moment that's too strange to capture—in words, with paint—but who can recognize it nonetheless, who will not be caught like a dumb animal but who can see the future, change it, who can see the past. I have yet to see a realistic image of the bombings or the aftermath, and his art is no exception. Yet it's the *pikadon* in my hands that makes me realize that it has never been their lack of words, or any failing in my interpreters, that holds me separate from the *hibakusha*. It is *a* lack of words.

But the tears will tell me.

The tattered fabric in Tokita-san's fingers. His dead sister's clothes.


|

## NOVEMBER 13, 2001

|


WHAT IF THE ANSWER is not in words, but not in silences either? If it is not in labels, nor facts, nor lies?

What if the answer is in the pictures?

The *hibakusha*'s pictures are children's pictures. They are scratches, squiggles; they look nothing like what must have been real. The adult mind tries to block the nightmare so it's the children within the *hibakusha* who must keep trying to tell the story, the mewling finger-painter who has learned to never temper pain. When Tokita-san paints the mushroom cloud in endless series, each one is different. Each one, if you put words to it, is orange, roughly the same shape and size, each a poor copy of the previous and an even poorer representation of the day. But what if the point is *not* to copy?

When I ask the *hibakusha* to describe the explosion, they

tell me: *It was red; It was black; Everything was grey; I couldn't see a thing. It was like a rainbow, so many swirling colors; I only saw the smoke later; It was the most beautiful sight anyone will ever see.* I have assumed all these answers are true, factual, that they can be mapped somehow, snapshots arranged according to age or location or timing. But Tokita-san's artwork points to many visions and interpretations, even within the same heart. He points, not to the facts, but to the feeling.

IN THE MONTHS BEFORE I left Brooklyn, I remember I spent a morning at Ian's primary school. The children were drawing, and they were so proud of their pictures; they would point to each scribble and tell me what it was. They had an impulse to create, and need to share, and if it looked nothing like a dog, nothing like what is "real," it didn't matter because they were young enough to believe in their own visions. I remember asking—"Where are his eyes?" "Is this his tail?" "How many legs does your dog have?"—telling them that the goal of art, of drawing, is to replicate as closely as possible what we all agree we see. Now, the voice in my head is Ian's, repeating what I never fully understood: *"Mommy, if you give me a pen, I will show you what the inside of my imagination looks like."*

The inside of us, and what it looks like. This is what I overlooked, even as I have always understood that I can conjure the truest stories with my own imagination. My imaginary narratives, their imaginary pictures—these are what move us, unedited, this is the experience that is "mine."

I know now what I was hearing before September 11: it was the story from a distance, a chorus of what "we" did, and also "he" and "she" and "they." It was nicely digested, put away. But it was fragile. In the face of a global trauma, an "I" emerged. If I go back, circle the pronouns, even in translation, I can trace the shift. Each individual found himself standing inside his own narrative, opened, once again, to his own experiences. As the man who finally gave up his famous anger showed me:

*"If I try to talk about it, to put it another way, the flash and the absolutely terrible . . . to try to convey it in a single word, our experience of the war as children, it was a poor . . . hard . . . scary . . . life."*

How we tell our stories makes all the difference. They are where we store our tears, where the eventual healing lies. If "we" are talking, then we are safe in our group perspective; we do not have to own our experience alone, nor do we have to feel it. What September 11 gave to the *hibakusha*, and what they gave in turn to me, is a way to re-enter memory. As scary, and painful, as it is to claim our pronouns, "we" cannot inhabit our own lives until "I" begins to speak.

**Subject: From Ian**
**To: Mom**

I miss you. I'm at Auntie's, we're listening to Prince. I called you not very long ago. When I called you, I felt like I missed you really much. Max is my best friend in school. We play in the block area. (Raspberry Beret just came on.) Ms. Debbie is my teacher's name. My brother is playing. If you forgot his name, I am going to write it down—Dylan. He is dancing like a maniac! Now he's shaking his booty. I have a boo-boo on my big toe, I kicked my soccer ball too hard, now I have a Band-Aid on it. Now Dylan is jumping on Auntie's bed. Bye mom.

Love, your son Ian

"My two sons, they were five and seven, were walking together to their grandmother's house when the bomb dropped and they got trapped under the wreckage of the falling buildings. Toshi threw himself over his little brother to protect him, but still, Ken died first. And after that, Toshi stopped speaking. He survived for a few more days, but I believe he really had nothing to say.

"I carried Ken's body to the cremation site in a bureau drawer. There were so many mounds of bodies, some more than three meters high. I didn't want to put him in one of those piles. I begged for wood, asking the officer in charge to please understand a parent's feelings. I put the drawer on an iron plate, and faced him with his head toward Danbara, where we lived, so that I would recognize his bones. But when Toshi died, the Lieutenant in charge was very stubborn and he made me leave the body next to the mound of bodies in front of the station. When I got there the next morning to pick up the ashes, Toshi's body was only half burned. I didn't tell my wife for years.

"It just wasn't something she could bear."

—Eighty-five-year-old male survivor

|
## NOVEMBER 14, 2001
|

She had two sons, ages five and seven, and now they are gone. She left them, and they died. She went to do some volunteer work in place of her neighbor, and that's why her sons were killed. No one else in Danbara died. She went to work that day; they were walking hand in hand to their grandmother's house . . . she can add details or strip facts.

The fact remains.

For the last half an hour, we have been talking while we waited for the TV crew to leave. The crew needed footage of me doing an interview for a story about my research, and it has been torture to have them here. Ken and Toshi live in this room, forever children; they look down from a life-like portrait, they gaze at their mother, they keep her real. Their lives are just as bright, their deaths just as raw to their father, but she is the one revealing her scars from the bomb-ing, the one who can wrap my heart in their final silence so completely I can no longer hear my own questions. I worry I will cry and the producer will try to stay longer; I worry that this woman will skim through her memories to keep her tears off TV. But mostly, I can feel that, for the first time ever, my defenses are being met—embraced and coddled, not with a soothing whitewash, but with an even greater sorrow. When I sat with Tokita-san, I could feel him drop the barrier between himself and his experience, but with this woman, it's the boundary between the two of us that is not there. I am open to the world behind my own protections, and suddenly I am the one who might burst into tears.

I am steering. Blind, but steering. Do you remember the first time you laughed after the boys died? The first beautiful image? These questions are safe for TV, but important. When does life begin again?

She doesn't remember.

The crew is gone, thanked profusely and now waiting outside. They know I will be another hour, but they'll stand in the cold in the courtyard to find out how it went. I sag in their absence, me and the elderly couple, pushing ninety: two people who are bent, frail, shrunken, grey, with failing eyesight and a hearing aid; old folks you might help to cross the street, but whom you would never imagine were witnesses to the beginning of the end of the world, or the keys to its future. They are the oracle, but they are also two sad people reliving their loss because a strange woman has appeared and asked them to. Their importance to the world ebbs when the camera crew leaves. I will resurrect it later, but for now, their greater gift is their humanity.

I sit beneath the painting of Ken and Toshi, myself the mother of two small boys, two years apart. Their own mother is crying, we are all beyond comfort. Beyond words. This story has become my own: my own pain, my own healing. How do I ask the unaskable?

*How will I keep living if it happens to my children?*

How will any of us survive the next attack?

It's been almost five months since I saw my sons. Yesterday, or was it several days ago?, I got a "breaking news" email from CNN that another airplane had crashed in New York. And the fear, the worry, the loneliness, and the abrupt and selfish thought that this might give me a reprieve from the potential disaster of my reunion with Brian all collided as I wondered: *Should they cancel their visit? Is it too much risk?* Released from his dormant anger—as I allowed myself to be just for a moment, just for that brief, fantastic maybe—I could imagine their fragile bodies in the sky. Just them, my little family: bones and skin and smiles and sleepy hugs. With no barriers, no protection, I could feel their excitement; I could imagine how much they wanted to see me, and I missed them so. Faced with the sudden specter that they might rise and never land, the uncertainty of their safety, I can suddenly feel how hard these months have been on all of us.

I have been away from my children too long. So far from my husband that neither of us knows what we will find once we are reunited. Brian said it was a bird in the propeller this time, not a terrorist, and I will choose to accept that because I need to. I will trust, because I love him, and we still have the time that the woman beside me lost when she left for work that August morning. And beneath the images of Ken and Toshi, arms around each other, I know for certain that that time is worth every risk we face.

# PART V
# ONE MUST ASK
# WHOSE?

*We shall not cease from exploration*

*And the end of all our exploring*

*Will be to arrive where we started*

*And know the place for the first time.*

—*T.S. Eliot*

# THE FAMILY ARRIVES

GOLDEN HAIR, BOWL-CUT, and oddly pastel eyes. My two sons, in Crayola sweatshirts and baggy jeans to match their father, and their father himself—my husband—towering above even the few foreigners in the stream of passengers pouring out of the customs exit around him. In motion, all of them: a rangy zigzag, hands, ankles, heads falling off the spine as they spin around and drift in the arrivals area, looking for me. I wave to them from the counter where I am in the act of spending one hundred dollars on train tickets back into the center of Tokyo, but their eyes slip over me, if indeed they swung in my direction.

They look good: unfamiliar; so familiar; unbelievable. As if they are not quite real, and not quite guaranteed, still they have materialized, whole and safe and tired and just slightly different. When at last my husband pulls my more Caucasian features from the crowd and throws up his hands just as I finish getting the tickets and turn toward them—*there she is!* his fingertips say, flung in my direction—the boys, too, catch sight and we are converging: my sons in a run, the three of them shaking off the distinct paleness of thirteen hours on a plane, and me just shaking. I kneel down and am pelted, for the space of a big, brief kiss, in bodies that are heavier than I remember, which press hard and release swiftly. My sons slide away, checking spaces, size, looking for bathrooms, before I can record them.

*Hey, Mom, hey, Mom. Cool hair. How come you're so tall?*

There is always a warning, and it comes when I stand; the first shot—a stiffness in Brian's hug announcing itself as an edge of anger that I was not here when they arrived, or at least not waiting, not pressed against the ropes as he imagined. In a more peaceful time, I might protest that I *was* here, challenge the definitions of his words; I might tell him of my own journey from Hiroshima: leaving the city on the six a.m. train, getting lost in Asakusa looking for our hotel where I went first to drop off my own bags so I could carry theirs and make sure there was in fact a room, and then lost again on the Yamanote line and barely making the airport express to meet their flight. Or maybe that is not the problem. Maybe it's the hair my children mentioned, which is curling in Japan's humidity, or the shoes? I look down, taking inventory, trying to remember where I bought these black, blocky boots with two inch heels, trying to remember if I wore heels before I left, if I was tall. My boys are taller, thicker, and more meaty in their clothes, our height differences have diminished in five months, but was it in Muji or the Greenwich Village Peddler that I bought these shoes?

Would it matter?

"How was the flight?"

It's not an urgent question, but I don't know where to start. Any topic, even *How are you?* is fraught, seems too big for the space we have, does not, in the reflection of Brian's face, seem safe. With the length of the flight confirmed between us—the longest trip my children have ever taken—and the assurance that it was fine, I take in their mountain of luggage. Three huge duffel bags, none of which, when I test them, I can lift. None of which have wheels. I seem to have forgotten there is such a thing as luggage without wheels, let alone that we owned so much of it.

We are not going straight home to Hiroshima. I have made a plan to stop along the way: we will make the best of the grand or so the train tickets are going to cost; we will meander, through Kyoto, where I have secured a reading to pay for part of our vacation, and then to Nara. I want them to fall in love, to see the beauty of Japan as soon as possible. I know I mentioned this to Brian and asked him to put everything they needed for the week into a single bag we could carry, but it seems that that was impossible, or incorrectly articulated, because when I ask which bag we are taking, and which will be sent on to Hiroshima by *takkyubin*, everything is mixed up, or not enough choices could be made in the chaos of getting out of New York, so the choices must be made here, in the arrivals area of Narita airport, near the window next to the *takkyubin* counter.

The boys have returned from the bathroom and are playing King of the Mountain on the luggage. I don't know which one of us moved, or whether we both did, but Brian is standing on the opposite side of the bags, waiting for me to take over, to pull the children off the luggage and, apparently, to repack everything. I am on the other side.

Brian watches as I busy myself, pulling open all three bags at once, stacking stuffed bears and blankets that we must have for security even though, as I explain to the boys—or is it begging?—we will all be sleeping together on the floor in the same room, along with short pajamas for the son who is always too hot and long pajamas for the other one and several pairs because they will only sleep in fresh ones. Every item becomes a requirement of living I am unused to, and it becomes immediately clear why there is no single bag packed and ready, even as it should be clear to them that some choices will need to be made. Underwear, socks, outer clothes and jackets, and toothbrushes go in the bottom of the bag, and everything else must fit according to priority or meet us at home. The boys protest the loss of their books, their extra hats, but they are more interested in playing tug of war with their sweatshirts and flinging each other onto the floor of the airport.

I work quickly. I don't look up to catch the eyes that will tell me I should not be repacking in the airport—of course I should not be repacking in the airport!—because there is no choice and I know no one will approach a gaijin directly to stop me. I don't look at Brian. When I woke up this morning and put on the black flared pants I bought in the Shareo in Hiroshima, the plain dark blue Uniqlo t-shirt that brings out my eyes, I was creating the first image he would have of me in months: someone to be proud of—my strength, my happiness—someone who could reassure him with my smile. Now, I wonder what he sees, whether I am as different as he is, more different than I can see myself, where the armor he is clad in comes from, and whether I have it too. Looking down on me now, on my industry, perhaps he will see me, let his gaze shift from whatever he might have expected—a vision from a hot New York June?—to who I am here. If I don't look up, I can imagine that transformation is beginning. If I look into the future, to Brian almost killing himself trying to carry the stripped down version of his luggage—a single fifty-pound duffel bag—as well as one of two unwakeable and comparably weighted boys out of the train station and through the night of Asakusa, I believe I am helping by stripping them of their habitual appendages: I am lightening his load. Brian waits until I'm finished and helps me drag what I've culled to the counter.

I smile at the agent, pretending he didn't just see me strew my family's life all over the airport floor. *Ano, sumimasen . . .* I begin. *Nitmotsu wa okuritain desu ga . . .*

Two more minutes and it's just us, on our way.

## | EXPLOSION |

THIS IS HOW LITTLE BOY, the bomb that was dropped on Hiroshima, was assembled: inside the shell, on opposite ends of the barrel, two pieces of uranium were placed, each smaller than the "critical mass" needed for fission. A conventional explosive forced the two together once the bomb was released. As soon as the critical mass was exceeded, it touched off a chain reaction that released energy equivalent to fifteen thousand tons of TNT in a millionth of a second, which, in turn, emitted powerful heat and radiation, expanded the surrounding air, and created a tremendous blast. The ingredients were all there, all individually harmless, but when they came together, it was as if the sky itself had exploded.

## | GAGAKU |

DAY FIVE, KYOTO, and I am surrounded by the wail of spirits trapped, a sound that is jarring, not so much in its dissonance, as in its sorrow. I am alone in our room at the *ryokan* for one more precious hour, drinking *maccha* with my walkman playing. I have returned early from my reading and am compulsive in my need for this thick, powdered tea used in the tea ceremony, which I have only tasted once before, and the squeal of the *shō*—the harmonic, multitiered mouth organ that strikes like a fistful of knives, carving loss into my head until my mouth waters. If I am forcing this experience, if I am looking to Japan itself to soothe me—its eccentricities and traditions, its instruments and tea—it doesn't matter. I can still forget, for the moment, that the shower doesn't work and see only the *shoji* doors and the enclosed balcony onto the inner courtyard. The seats out there are too rickety to sit on, and the balcony floor is plastic tile, but the low table where I am sitting is very much like the one I have in Hiroshima. There is a Noh mask, and a simple *tokonoma* altar, and a kabuki doll in a glass box resting on the safe that doesn't seem to work. In the mid-afternoon, there is nowhere to walk. When Brian and the boys left the *ryokan* to explore Kyoto while I was working, they left three futons and all the bedding all over the floor. If I fold them, it will be a rebuke, but I am too tired to care.

I can't write. I am trying, in this sudden solitude, but there's nothing on the page.

AFTER FIVE DAYS HERE, the boys still think Japan is not so different from New York. It's just the same, they tell me, except New York has no temples. New York also has no shrine weddings, no *yukata*s, squat toilets, tatami floors, futon beds, pillows stuffed with beans, hand held shower "rooms," toilets in a separate cubicle, no-shoes rules, rice and soup for breakfast, *senbei* stores, fresh red bean *anko* cakes, *yakitori* everywhere in the streets, *taiko* drums . . . This is the world I have been living in—my new world; these are the experiences I've tried to cram into their first week. This is my gift—my eyes, my vision culled from my full five months in Japan—and the pain I feel when they toss it aside is startling. How can they not love what I love? How can they not even see it?

Brian points out that the buildings here are not as big as the ones in New York, and that, here, the taxis aren't yellow.

This is the culture shock: fragmented, lodged in the skin. We keep knocking against our differences—Brian sees them before I do; he draws the conclusions. I am rejecting him when I try to keep the boys from treating the *shinkansen* like an amusement park; when I feel the stiff backs of the quiet Japanese families and the unprecedented sight of passengers leaving their assigned seats to move to another car on the train; when I connect it to the fact that my children are singing the soundtrack of *Shrek* at the top of their lungs. It is true that I'm so aware of our perpetual uproar: our huge bags in the streets, our need for something sweet in the morning and for a toilet in our room. They look askance at the foods I reach for; they wait, bouncing, for the world to move in those moments when I would wait for time to spin down. I feel as if I'm floating, and I don't know if I was floating before they came, when I was living a life where I was doing "nothing" as Brian points out, or if I am hovering now because I haven't yet found a hook on their lives to attach to. It's as if we have lost a common field of vision:

when we reach out to the place where we think we see each other, there is only air.

I can do no right—not yet. Not when I'm with them, not when I must leave them, which I did on our second night together, after a long day of sightseeing, when they were hungry but too tired to sit in a restaurant. Dylan was sniffling, too jetlagged to open his eyes; we had only *sembe* in our hotel room—puffed air wrapped in seaweed—and Brian cannot speak the language so it was left to me to bring home dinner for my brood.

Take-out seemed an obvious choice, though I don't know who suggested it. That is, until I found myself alone in an unfamiliar town, learning the hard lesson that Japanese restaurants don't generally have disposable containers, until I found myself searching farther and farther from the hotel, stretching time past the breaking point until I finally walked into a small eating place, so flustered by then—so aware of my failures that I couldn't make myself understood, all those words I thought I'd learned, where were they when I needed them?—that the cook abandoned his kitchen, asked his diners for their patience, and escorted me down the street and right, then left, then pointed me to a distant food stand. There, where the owner was about to close down, I could buy a stewed fish head and stewed *gobo* and some other items, like seaweed salad, that my children have never eaten. It was food, the only food I had found in the last forty minutes, and they were starving. I tried to imagine them in our hotel room—soft and hard, small and large and always warm, and hungry—and so ill-equipped to pick up a fish head and suck on it. Could they do it? Would they? Might they accept that I had done my best, that this was Japan, and eat the only thing I could offer? As the woman stacked the most innocuous items into two bags for me, why was it that the only image I could conjure was of my two sons climbing on their father, curled up against, around and under, their faces pressed into his skin and so far away from me? I used all the money I had left in my wallet after a day of endless spending on the family and took a different route back to the hotel. There it was, a block away: 7-Eleven. The chain where I have bought half of my meals in Hiroshima, a place my stunned brain had entirely forgotten.

THEY WILL BE BACK SOON, back from the train museum where they spent their time during my reading—too boring for the boys to attend in Brian's judgment. That their day went well is more important than the result of my own. Last night, with the boys laid out on futons and the two of us huddled in the corner of the hotel room with only the shower stall to retreat to, Brian protested—frustrated and frazzled—at the prospect of having the boys on his own again. *Why do you have to do this reading?* he asked. *What are we supposed to do alone in Kyoto?*

How fast this happens.

*I didn't come here to babysit.*

I knew he didn't come here to babysit. Of course he didn't. They have been without me for 150 days. Why would they want to be alone for one minute longer? How can they navigate Japan, a place even I'm finding more difficult than

I thought it was? I gave them an English map of Kyoto, took them to the English tourist bureau; I circled the sights, explained the buses. I gave Brian my guidebook, dog-eared on all the pages he would want to read, but I could feel his resistance every time I flipped one: not wanting to embrace my interests, not ready yet to find his own.

I have amends to make. For 150 days, he sacrificed and now it's my turn. That's why I made the promise. This reading will be my last official bit of work. If it is faith we are missing, I have offered something to hold onto: I will put my book aside, let Japan be our playground. All of us together as a family, after this reading, which I have just finished, never alone.

|

## NIGHTINGALE FLOORS

|

MY SON IS CRAWLING on the floor.

Not in our hotel, on our tatami, quietly toward the door so his father won't wake up. Not in the otherwise-childless *izakayas*, the pubs in which we have to weave our way past drinking patrons to go to the bathroom for the third time.

No, he is crawling in the castle, the jam-packed World Heritage Nijo castle in Kyoto, four hundred years old, former home to the Shoguns, an estate that was once so grand the rocks themselves were oriented to provide the most pleasing view. It is a paranoid's dream of moats and towers and high walls and secret rooms—much of which is closed to the public—but the main palace is a playground for my children, both of whom are crawling, and slithering under the "no entry" ropes, perilously close to the sliding shoji doors that protect the lord's inner chambers and the priceless, gilded paintings of tigers, animals, waterfalls, and other natural beauty deemed too delicate for a photo flash.

If I could pretend the boys weren't mine, I might try, but although we are three of thousands of tourists—this is the height of the fall foliage, and *kinrou kansha no hi*, a vacation that has been described to me as "thanks for your labor, now go out and commune with the trees," which every Japanese citizen must have decided to do in the Kansai region because it was hell getting a room in Kyoto during the week and tomorrow there is no room at any inn in Kyoto, Nara, or Osaka, nothing as far west as Okayama, so tomorrow we have to go home to Hiroshima earlier than I planned—still, today, in this castle, we are the only white people here. The boys could never get lost; tens, even hundreds, of helpful Japanese would immediately usher them to join me wherever I disappeared to, but that is not why I'm stuck to them. I'm stuck to them by the knowledge that they are *fast*. Fast enough to be past the sliding doors and grubbily fingering the painted tigers if I so much as turn around. And there is no refuge in Brian either, since I owe him five months of downtime and he's spending only his first morning of it now while I try to cope with these nightingale floors. All morning, my children have been fine—decently behaved if a little vigorous—but coming up on midday these floors, which were built deliberately to squeak so no assassin could sneak up on the Shogun, have turned them into samurai. It is an undeniable challenge for two dark blond boys in red down coats who like to shriek, and laugh, and who are now dragging themselves on their hands. It's an unimaginable challenge for me that Dylan has just become some strange creature named Jonal while I get a guilty glimpse into how hard Brian's world has been, and he is contemplating the peace of a golden temple I have never seen.

They crawl; they run; they've been in Japan a week now and I've never seen them walk, not even to the shower. They favor the castles for the "keep out" ropes they try to swing on; in the gardens, they will kiss me and hug me and tell me they love me and then duck the barriers and try to jump into the ponds. I am thanking the Japanese Tourist Bureau for closing three quarters of this compound to the public. To say that I'm not used to ages three and five is the world's most pathetic understatement. Three and five year olds do not sightsee; they do not even see sights unless it is the sight of all the small pebbles they can lob at each other, which hit the bent-over *obaasans* between them each time they miss. My "mother shock" is characterized by my complete inability to keep old ladies safe from my children.

*Ian!*

I'm not Ian, I'm Ash.

And I'm Brock, Dylan declares. And you're Misty.

If Pokemon characters are not national treasures, at least they are Japanese.

Ian yells for "roll call," which apparently requires each of us to answer to our Pokenames, and for the last to say: "All present and accounted for." They want me to tell them how to say this in Japanese.

I don't know.

*Mina-san wa iimasu yo.*

Maybe. Possibly. It's the best I can do, and I can't tell whether people are staring because we are mangling Japanese at a refresh rate of once every ten seconds, because our dragging sneakers are writing illiterate but complex political treaties in accidental kanji in the dust, or simply so the pebbles won't hit them between their shoulder blades again. Castles, temples, shrines, pagodas—all of these are crowded out of my day's itinerary by two thoughts. The first one is that under no circumstances do I want to risk assault charges by retracing my steps back into the castle even for a forgotten fleece hat, and the second is: ducks. The boys love ducks and there must be a park somewhere. We still have three, unimaginably long hours before we are supposed to meet Brian at the *ryokan*.

We'll walk, I decide, to tire them out.

We walk, and keep walking. We are looking for a bus, but I am navigating Kyoto with a map that's entirely out of scale, and, by the time we cram ourselves into the rear door of one and try to figure out the idiosyncrasies of how to pay the fare, my body is as weary as my shell-shocked mind. We dump ourselves off at a park, where I can't find the promised ducks. Ian and Dylan are scrambling in the gravel path in front of me, and, whatever their game is, it is turning into a fight. Something about Captain Hook—Dylan doesn't want to be Captain Hook—and when I tell Ian to stop bugging his brother, he calls me a fish face. I couldn't care less about being a fish face, but Dylan doesn't like this at all—being a fish face is a bad thing, unacceptable especially for his mother, and since he is three and correspondingly powerless, he is crying. The tears provoke more of a "sing" in the song of "fish face," which Dylan meets with screams of *No!* and some stamping. Any minute he's going to throw himself into the gravel in my defense. I am beyond nurture, beyond compassion and reason. I need a diversion, so even though I know I shouldn't reward bad behavior, I pull a box of chocolate-covered Pockys out of my backpack and rediscover one of the golden rules of maternal sanity: Feed the children.

No wonder their behavior has fallen off so impossibly. It is two p.m., and I have completely forgotten lunch.

# RUNNING

I DREAM HER RUNNING. Footsteps on the stairs below.

I am standing in a stairwell, in a building I have never seen: barren, shattered walls. A relic, or under construction; there is a sky here. A blue sky. It's my mother on the stairs, ascending. Something in the sound I recognize: she is rushing toward me and I'm waiting to catch her in my arms. Because it is a dream, I can know this is why I'm here. It's up to me to scoop her out of the stream she is caught in. She cannot stop.

When her face rises at the level of my feet and I see it for the first time, her eyes are wide, pinned back, panicked, her hair flying away from her head as if she is falling, though she's rushing in the opposite direction. The wrong direction, impossible, but I know it is her, even though she looks nothing like herself. She is a cartoon, a spooked horse; her terror startles me and so she's past me before I can catch her, ahead of me on the stairs, and before I can move—I'm not frozen, just dumb, just unable—the stairs begin to crumble, each stair she has touched falling away and I'm in a hall suspended in space, the sky in front and beneath and above me, the stairs falling.

I do not know if I can't, or won't, or didn't follow. All I'm aware of is the ringing footfalls of my mother above me running up the endless, crumbling stairs.

## SACRIFICES

IT IS NOT UNTIL it happens that you realize it has been happening all along—like my telephone ringing when we get back to Hiroshima, so many requests and invitations. When did I collect so many people in my life, and how could I have thought myself alone with all these calls? If, in my first weeks in Hiroshima, I was having trouble rummaging up a single interview, now they are pouring in. How could I have believed myself unproductive when I've done so much and there's so much more to do?

Although it seems torn from the pages of fiction, a woman I called during my first week here has suddenly decided she's ready to talk to me. I remember that first contact, my inability to secure a yes and her offer of tea. Now, I can't remember what her story was, and whether I have "gotten" it already. This calculation is more than ugly— my encounters with the *hibakusha* have become a kind of healing, less about my own need for information than about their re-experiencing the bomb in safety—and I'm not sure where it comes from. I've been in Japan long enough to have mastered my own demur: my family is here. Perhaps there might be time later, yes, when it is convenient.

I wish it could be true.

I have gotten into the habit of letting the phone ring, then checking my messages. A man I spoke with last month, who treated me to a five-course lunch made entirely from tofu so that he could lay out his full argument in favor of a Japanese "fighting force," now wants to take me to see the kamikaze museum in Kagoshima, at the southernmost tip of Japan. He has called three times in the last week, and I have not answered. I can feel myself pulling away, though I don't know what from, exactly; there's a disconnect in my life I will not look at, but that I expect will become clear.

Meanwhile, I am home, returning only those calls I can say yes to. Which are Jane and Kimiko—*Yes, we are home safe. I will see you soon*—and Ami.

Ami calls in the evening, after Brian is asleep. Her father will be performing again. This time, he wants to invite us backstage. And the doctors she's been trying to reach for me have suggested a time when we can meet. There are two of them, friends, men who were working in the Red Cross Hospital when the bomb fell. One of my characters is a doctor, and I have always said I need to understand how they moved in the world during the war and how they coped with the bombing, that I need to be able to describe the inside of crumbled buildings, where the dead, dying, and damaged were indistinguishable for weeks. It has taken more than a month for Ami to get these two men together, but she has done it at last and she's bursting with the news.

I haven't told her about my promise to Brian. Every time I try, the words sound wrong. *He doesn't want me to. I need to be with them.* It makes no sense that I'm in Japan but *not* doing interviews, though when I made this offer, in Kyoto, it seemed like the only choice.

When we were apart, Brian did everything. He refused all help; he made cookies for the school bake sale instead of buying them like the rest of the working parents; he cooked for the children *and* my parents every night of their month-long visit instead of getting takeout. Instead of doing what I begged him to: go out, go away for the weekend, take a photography course, try to relax. He hollowed himself out, inspired by his friends' comments that he was "a saint" to let me go to Japan, rehearsing the shorter fact that *he was letting me do this*. It was his gift to me, and the harder it was to give, the more proof that he loved me; the more synergy he could create—however postponed and long distance—to bind us together when we were reunited.

It *was* a gift. It was for me. But in its giving, both of us are miserable. There's no gesture I can make to match it, not even giving up my interviews. He has no faith, not in me, not in my promises. Anything I do for myself now just throws his sacrifices in his face.

Even when he's asleep—as they all are now, my childhood sweetheart on his back, arms out like Christ ascending, a small boy tucked into each crook—Brian's cheeks are sunken and his eyes bruised by his long ordeal. While I was in the shower, playing these same, terrible grooves in hope of an answer, *Charlie and the Chocolate Factory* folded itself around his exhausted thumb and in less than five minutes, the three of them lost the bedtime story and drifted away. The thing I do not forget, cannot forget, amid Brian's distress and the boys' wild sally forth on their saucers of need, is that I love them. I chose them.

"Brian . . . " I say into the telephone. There must be some way to make Ami understand. "He's so tired and he's had the kids for so long . . . "

"Of course he can come too," she says. She means to the Noh performance. In true Japanese fashion, she has heard my words, but more than that, she's heard my silence and she understands this is serious. While I've been running through my mind, she has been spinning a plan. Has he seen

Tomo-no-ura? she asks. Of course, there's been no time, not yet. But he could go there, while I am doing my interview. He could rent a bike—it's a beautiful fishing village with narrow streets on the Inland Sea, so easy to navigate—and of course someone else will watch the children. She will fix it. It is set then. He will love it. He will love Japan.

I can't suggest this to Brian. I know what Ami's saying to me, that I have put her in an awkward situation, that she will lose her credibility if I say no. I know the reputation she has been building with me is important to her work as a peace activist, and that she believes these interviews will save the world. This is what she's telling me, with her forcefulness. I am being squeezed on both sides and I don't know if there's any leeway on either. I know something else too, even as I take in my sleeping family: there is yet another interview I've been trying to arrange, the most important interview of my time here, and I have recently received an email that it might come through.

I can't fight this. I don't know what to do, except to do nothing.

"Why don't you call back in the morning?" I ask her. "You can say hello to Brian. He is so looking forward to meeting you."

|

# BACK STAGE AT THE NOH THEATER

|

FIFTEEN MINUTES BEFORE show time, and Ami has slipped
me behind the great stage curtain, where we can watch her
father getting ready for his role. The first play is the story
of the moon princess who comes down to earth to bathe in
a pool and the fisherman who steals her robe. Ami's father
plays the goddess; he is seated in a wide chair, draped in
a kimono and *hakama* of gold and orange. The costume,
deliberately bulky, is being tweaked into perfect drapes by
the dressers who are helping him get into his role. The fab-
rics swirl in a cacophony of colors and patterns; the final,
clashing layer of orange and gold is perhaps deliberately too
brilliant to hold the human eye.

If Brian was here, would he see it as I do? Would the
Japanese indifference to coordinated clothing that's evident
daily on the street of Hiroshima flicker into his head? This
is joy for me, crazy as it seems—these fleeting glimpses of
sense that pass through whenever I'm not trying to make
sense. When I first came to Japan, I would have analyzed
this clothing preference, written a little paragraph on it; just
before Brian came, I would have experienced it and let it go.
Though I can guess, I'll never know which reaction Brian
would have to this. We couldn't bring the children, so Brian
wouldn't come.

The goddess ignores us and the fussing dressers. He is
gazing at his reflection in the full-length mirror that's been

placed in front of him. On his head, an elaborate female hair-piece, and over it, in front of his face, a spray of ornamental gold. The goddess's mask is set quite high—her forehead above his, which leaves quite a fat lower jaw protruding and gives his silhouette a hunched appearance.

Ami's father is still, absorbing his reflection. No effort has been made to hide this man inside his character, and yet he's disguised just the same. This effect is noticeable on the stage, but up close, enough to see his pores and jowls, something I have come to sense about Japan suddenly comes into focus. I remember, when I first arrived here, being preoc-cupied with opposites and lies. How could we claim one thing, yet be another? Americans view 'duality' as decep-tion: they pride themselves on being transparent, on being one thing—only and always—and turning that "true" face to the world. The Japanese, though, show their allegiance to society, and their respect, by being different in the outside world than they would be at home. In Japan, dichotomy is commonplace, and yet it is less like division, and more like addition. We can be both indirect and forceful; victim and savior; mother, yet child. We prize the Noh dancer because we can see the essence of both creatures—the heavy body moving lightly—and we understand the achievement.

His feet make her step mincing. His fan flickers with her grace. We want to see his skill beneath her face and hold onto both at the same time.

Him and her, simultaneous. Both visible. Both real.

|

# CONSULTING WITH DOCTORS

|

ON THE DAY BEFORE, we tiptoe. When we walk together to the train station to buy his tickets to Tomo-no-ura, to get film for his camera, I point out the stairs to the platforms and confirm the number of the one where he will wait in the morning. Brian is more like himself today, the former intrepid traveler. I write down a few basic questions for him in Japanese—*jitensha wa . . . doko desuka?*—so he can rent a bicycle to get around and he mutters them, testing and tasting the words. I don't know how Ami did it, but he seems excited to be going out on his own. He has decided to be happy, to enjoy Japan, and if the day means that I will also be enjoying a different, separate Japan, he seems to have accepted that for the moment.

We do not voice the fact that I am doing an interview when I said I would not. We do not declare it the last one.

And on that morning, Ian wakes up just as Brian is leaving and comes into my room to snuggle under my futon. We lie together and look through the gauzy curtains to the river. I give him a hug and he whispers: "I love you, Mommy." Then turns his head and pukes all over my pillow.

The front door is opening. I wait until it closes.

The interview is not until noon. The interval between vomiting is getting longer, but Ian can't hold water down. He's so tired he will curl up on the linoleum floor of his own volition, which is a good thing since I can't put him in the tatami rooms or under the quilted and borrowed *kotatsu* in case he vomits again, so I lay a towel down on the linoleum, cover him with blankets, and pull the small space heater over to him.

He sleeps.

I think.

Dylan devours two pre-manufactured pancakes from 7-Eleven, one squashed chocolate pudding *manju* shaped like a fish, a banana, and toast.

I could live without this interview if I had to. My child is sick, and my work is much less important that he is. But . . . the boys have shown a great capacity to puke and recover within hours. Ian will spend his day sleeping. And Brian is gone.

I circle this dawning conclusion, poised to cast it off if it's revealed to be too self absorbed. But it sits there. Inert. *No one is pressing me, or angry to be picking up my slack, so why am I even questioning whether I should drop the interview for a bad bite of chicken or a touch of the flu?*

I am losing the novel. Once my story haunted me, but now I've handed it over, tried to buy peace with it, even though I know it's not the right currency and peace cannot be bought. I ignored the bombing once, and I am doing it again, numbly putting it off to the side until my life is more stable, focusing instead on our travel schedule, waiting for that future day—"when nothing else is going on"—and hoping that I've already gathered everything I will need then. But what if I haven't? What if my memory fades, just as theirs has or through some other, more ominous manner?

What if I lose myself, and the book dies? I used to think I owed this book to my Aunt Molly. Then I owed it to the *hibakusha*, who tell their stories so that their loved ones will not have died in vain.

But now, I want it back. I miss my ghosts.

I call Ami and begin to broach the subject of the vomit. She's the one who will stay with the boys—they've met her and it seemed to be the best choice—so I've asked another friend to do my translation. She assures me she will come, no problem; she has friends with children, she has borrowed lots of toys and books—so many things to do at my house for the afternoon. Don't worry about the kids, don't worry about *Harry Potter*, the movie they will now no longer go to, don't worry that she'll get sick too . . . By the time Ami arrives, Ian has not thrown up in hours, though he's not eaten anything in hours either, and from his prone position, he even seems mildly interested in her wealth of goodies.

*Are you sure this is okay?*

Of course. Look at Dylan.

Dylan is already tossing his way through the pile of books, looking at the drawings. I promise to be back in two and a half hours.

Better make that three.

Dr. Yamada has a lot to say. So does his friend, Dr. Yoshida. So does Dr. Suzuki, the sister of another colleague who they call to join the interview about an hour into my visit. My translator is gamely trying to follow all three of them, sometimes in two overlapping conversations, when yet another of their friends drops by and she is a *hibakusha* too. The new arrival has brought fresh bread, which allows me a break to call and check on Ian (he seems okay, sitting up, holding down a bit of water but no food). I am an hour overdue, and Ami has to leave, but again, this is no problem, she will just take the boys to Kimiko's house.

Kimiko knows they are sick and doesn't care. She wants to have a pizza party.

It's a balancing act, but it seems to be working. The tape is rolling, and the discussion is still going in the other room. It's difficult to follow the simultaneous conversations, to decide which one to participate in and try to direct, and I'm not even sure who's saying what since it's all being channeled through my translator.

The windows were smashed, so they hung straw mats over the holes to try to keep out the flies. There were patients everywhere: on the floor, even on the ground outside without a futon to lie on, but it was so hot it didn't matter. Everyone was hurt, doctors and patients alike. I can see Dr. Yamada extracting glass fragments from his own body without anesthesia, but the image is gone before I can ask how many, from where, and whether it hurt. I can't smell the cremation, because no one else could—they are numb to most sensory input within days—but Dr. Yoshida is digging pits and piling bodies, and there's a bonfire of burning flesh just outside the building day and night.

The stories are flooding in from every direction, and I am catching what I can, absorbing what I can, trusting the tape recorder to catch the overflow: there is a clerk directing patients like traffic—he wears a headband and carries a sword, but was he a clerk at the hospital or somewhere else—and why the sword? A family heirloom saved from a falling building? Protection because the war is not yet over? Insanity? We are moving in and out of time and detail in a whirl that I have missed so much: the beds were iron frame; even before the bombing, hospitals had no emergency admission system, so people who were suddenly ill or injured had to be taken to the doctor in a two-wheeled, hand drawn cart. If only I had more time, or I could speak to each of them separately, then I could exhaust each story, but I am out of practice and this is the greatest challenge I have faced. I can feel their narratives fragmenting, shattering into a million points of view. I can't keep up, and yet, I am transcending, being restored: they are spinning the story back to life, painting the rainbow of visions and interpretations that remind me that the truth is somewhere, not in the details but in the heart of it, if I can just blur my focus and feel. They are returning my novel to me, and I am just so happy to be here.

After four hours, I can't stay any longer, although we're eating bread and cake and no one is moving to leave. I have to excuse myself due to a sick child. Dr. Suzuki is a pediatrician, and very concerned to hear about Ian since there's a severe flu going around and she has been hospitalizing children for dehydration. It's just as well that I didn't know about the severe flu; just as well I found out from a pediatrician who has offered free medication if I follow her to her clinic. So into the streets we go on two bicycles to get suppositories for the boys because of course, when kids are puking, they can't hold medicine in their stomachs so it has to go the other way. It means another twenty minutes, and it's just as well I don't know Ian has assured Kimiko that he can eat pizza, is in the process of eating three pieces as I ride, and is preparing to throw up in a spectacular manner in her *genkan* when I arrive.

I am a bad mother. I am a sloppy researcher. But at least I have been to the doctor.

"I went back to the hospital after the war ended, on the seventeenth of August. The ceiling had collapsed, the walls were broken down, the window glass was smashed into pieces. Chunks of rubble and plaster were gathered and put out of the way, but the facilities were completely destroyed. On the ground, just in front of the hospital building, a huge pile of dead bodies were being cremated.

"That was eleven days after the bombing. There were still patients everywhere, inside and outside the building. Where there were benches or any kind of furniture remaining, they were turned into beds, but the rest were lying on the floor. Since it was summer, they did not need futons. But the maggots—I was amazed by the great number of maggots and flies. On bodies, on food, on whatever you had. You could see the maggots moving inside people's wounds.

"I waded through them. Everyone helped. Soldiers, nurses, technicians, pharmacists, clerks, anyone who survived and could move. The doctors took charge in turn but there was no medicine, no medical supplies. People were asking for help—some were shouting, but in most cases, there were only low groans.

"It was unbearable."

—Seventy-six-year-old former
surgical intern, survivor

|

# NAMES ON A LEAF

|

WE ARE ON THE ROAD, on my first trip away from Hiroshima
that has nothing to do with my novel. We have planned it
for Brian, to add to the growing bag of film that he started
in the fishing village and ease his displeasure that I left
my sick son alone with a babysitter while he was gone. At
some unrecorded mile marker on the Seto Ohashi Bridge,
we entered uncharted territory, and I crossed the blessed
threshold between tour guide and tourist. We are now on
the northeast corner of the island of Shikoku, *sanuki udon*
country, land of thick noodles and thatched roofs and vine
bridges; it's the first place we have visited that I've never
seen and, therefore, am in no way responsible for. Here,
where there are no longer any expectations, and none of the
ideals I've been scrambling to meet, we can start over and
encounter Japan on equal footing. We are heading into the
heart of the island, toward Kompira-san, a shrine that sits
eight hundred steps above the sleepy, traditional village of
Kotohira.

Faith is returning, fueled from unexpected sources. At
the *ryokan* in Kotohira, my Japanese is not as spotty as it
seems: our hostess shows us the *furo* with no long explanation about how we are supposed to wash before getting
into it; her husband smiles and helps us find some palat-
able medicine when Dylan throws up without warning on
his shoes. All of this without the panic I first encountered

in the J-phone shop when I got to Hiroshima, without the panic I felt walking into the *okonomiyaki* building to find I was unable to order a meal. Now, I can tell our host we would like the usual Japanese breakfast and he believes me. A bit of rice and sweet rolled omelet for the boys (plus a leftover doughnut from the car), but this is Brian's first *wa choshoku*. He is game. We're the only foreigners in their dining room; the boys chime *itadakimasu* before eating, and Brian lifts a cradled cup in his palm to be served tea. The boys seem to view the deliberate array of food on the trays in front of them as a game, not as weird purple and yellow things. Everything goes down—rice, soup, pickled vegetables, sweet beans, *umeboshi*—from Brian's tray and the kids'. Brian even eats the stewed fish, and if he passes the little fermented ones my way, I still breathe a little deeper and smile more broadly at each bite. Had I asked him what he wanted for breakfast, or did I, as in my memory I will imagine it, make the decision and hope? The boys challenge their father, pointing to tiny fingerlets of dried fish on their own trays and he feigns impatience—who do they think he is that he would turn up his nose at a bit of fish skin?—but with his own smile, and I love him for it.

THERE ARE EIGHTY-EIGHT temples in Shikoku, or at least there is an eighty-eight temple walk, which takes two months and is supposed to bestow on the pilgrims who make the journey the ability to overcome the eighty-eight evil human passions defined in Buddhist doctrine. These days, the pilgrims often go by bus. Kompira-san is one of these sites, and the wide, granite steps to the top of Mt. Zozu are peopled with chipper folks equipped with hats and walking sticks; if you didn't bring your own, the souvenir shops and udon factories have stands full of them outside their doors—they are free loaners, and an incentive to stop on the way down to purchase *omiyage* or eat lunch. The shops step up with the stairs for nearly half the climb: it is a terraced mall where masks and snacks begin to run together. The path breaks into occasional plateaus; for all the talk of an arduous climb—and if 785 steps is not enough, there are actually more than five hundred more to get to the true end of the path at the inner shrine—there are so many levels with temples and halls and even a stable with horses, that no one breaks a sweat.

We meander. Our day flows into the gaps; buildings with no sign of life outside them are magnets for Brian. This is how we end up at the entrance to a museum, where the docent comes out personally to invite us to remove our shoes. Shoes have been another challenge since the family arrived, heavily outfitted in laces, but Brian and the boys want to see it, so I follow them up a sloping tatami floor in stocking feet to a table where we pay a thousand yen and get a brochure with reproductions of paintings of two tigers drinking and a beautiful series of cranes.

The museum reminds me of the castles and retreats we visited in Kyoto: wooden, with wide *engawa*—the sheltered wraparound porches and walkways—and tatami rooms with sliding paper doors that stand open so the paintings can be viewed without actually having to step inside. The boys like the tigers, but they are thrilled when our guide steps off the *engawa* and pulls a couple of leaves off a bush. He scratches a word into the leaf with a rock and within a minute, the leaf blackens around the cut and the word shows up clearly. Each boy gets to pick a leaf for his own name, and of course, Dylan wants to be the one who jumps into the garden to yank them off the bush. He is too young to write his name—he will oversee Ian's careful letters, but once he's sure the word is there, that he's part of the family of leaves, he is drawn to greater interests. He wants to dance in stocking feet on the ground and play with the rocks. There is a peace in the sound of the insects around him, buffeting his simple pleasure. I am still full of hope, full of our best morning yet in Japan and our unity as a family.

This feels like a place that my mother would love, a place where, if my boys were not so bustling, she might join me, her eyes closed, breathing deep, listening to the sound-track of tinkling water. I have come to expect her now. She has been with me in Japan almost daily, even in a passing thought that feels like a brush of her hand or a kiss on my forehead. It's not until then that I realize I've been living with my mother, and also that I haven't felt her once since my own children arrived.

She is missing.

"Mom? Are you okay?"

I can feel my eyes burning, become aware that they're closed. I can feel myself gasp, convulse really. Ian's voice brings me back. This is grief. I have to hold it inside me—it can't be too hard, I don't even know where it came from.

Maybe it's the stairs—I dreamed of my mother running up some stairs—but I don't know. I open my eyes; Ian has gone to get his father.

There is a family of leaves on the plank floor of the *engawa*. I imagine another one, written in childish letters, but would it say *Grandma*? Would Ian write her name? I consider these questions as if they were important, as if I was considering her signature on a contract. One that might say: *I will always be there*. I am listening for her, and suddenly so tired. I don't want to look up, don't want to go forward, I want my mother to return, to reassure me that she's still here, but of course, she is not and our visit is over: the docent is trying to corral Dylan in the garden as he hops from rock to rock, and Ian is tugging his father along.

Brian is watching me; I can feel him. I don't look up until I actually do feel him, moving forward to brush my shoulder, as if to ask, *Are you okay?* I don't know what Ian told him, but if Brian was frustrated before, if that was the expression I didn't want to see, now he looks as if he thinks I might truly be losing my mind.


WE WALK THE STEPS. For long stretches, we pretend we're a train, with a walking stick on either side sandwiching us into a line. Taking turns—who is the engine, who is the caboose, who gets to make the "whoo whoo" noise—and I can't even hear the birds. We march through the plazas, past the temples that I would have lingered on, to breathe. We swing around the corners, snapping the back end of the train as we pivot. I am going along; giving up, giving in. I feel so heavy, and so alone, but they don't seem to notice, except that I am lagging too much, not sounding loud enough.

*Come on, Mom. Don't let go.*

I don't want to be the train. I don't want to be the mother. I don't want to be the zookeeper, either, the responsible one who has already spent too much of their visit saying: "Don't pee in the *furo*. Don't run on the *shinkansen*. Don't jump up and down on the neighbors' ceiling. Don't touch." I did it to myself, I know: I am the one who pitted one against the other, put my family in opposition to my work. I am the one who offered not to do the interviews, never to leave my family alone.

But at this moment, childish as it is and selfish, I want some quiet. My mother is lost, and I am the mother now. I am not the woman she was, a mother who could make her child feel like there was nothing she would rather be doing than being with me, being my mother. No, I am a mother of peanut butter nightmares, unable to cope, unsure of when I began to feel so much and fall apart so easily.

The "whoo whoo" noise is pressing into my head. I want to stop. Turn around. Take the next five hundred steps and disappear. I want to freeze the boys in time so I can figure out what I'm supposed to do now. How do I take care of these needs when I have so many of my own?

"Whoo, whoo!"

The noise has changed, is now a challenge. Dylan is racing downhill, Ian trying to catch up behind him. They are galloping, heading for the next set of stairs; something terrible is about to happen and Brian and I both yell at them to stop. There's a man on the top of the stairs, directly in front of Dylan's charge. My son seems to be flying toward him, his feet cycling beneath him to keep up with his body's gravity. There is no way he's going to avoid hitting the man. I can see it in my mind's eye—bodies falling together, tumbling over each other down the long, stone stairs. I am waiting for the collision when suddenly Ian has overtaken his brother; he gets between them and throws his arm around Dylan just in time to swing him around the startled man. As I watch, Ian's body takes the momentum, absorbing it easily as the boys seem to dance together on what looks like the horizon. Then, without looking to us for approval, without even thinking, my young American son, the one with green eyes and dark blonde hair who never fails to take care of his little brother, says a word to beg the man's pardon, with perfect Japanese inflection:

"*Sumimasen!*"

The man bows slightly to my children as I begin to smile, and then the boys are gone—down the stairs.

"Then the war crimes trials started in Shanghai. We were told to interrogate this general, who was in charge of the Japanese military forces in Taiwan. He was very cooperative, very calm—it was winter and he was wearing a nice large overcoat. He requested that we release his men since he, because of his rank, was fully responsible for every act of the soldiers under him. We were all very impressed by him; he had none of the arrogance that you sometimes see. He said, 'You are officers and you know that a senior officer's order cannot be ignored, so whatever they did, they were ordered to do by me, and I will take responsibility for every act.'

"Then, that night, after he signed a full confession, he took out the arsenic that he had hidden in his coat and committed suicide.

"During the trials, there were several non-commissioned and commissioned officers—colonels, like that—who were convicted of torturing American airmen shot down over Shanghai and Taiwan. Some were given long-term prison sentences, and some were given the death sentence. There was a special wing where these prisoners were being held, and on the nights when they were having executions, all the Japanese prisoners in the wing would stand at attention in their cells, and when the man who was going to the execution chamber walked by, they would all sing this Japanese song . . . it's a war song, but a very quiet song, about a soldier: he is going to war and may never come back but he is doing it for his country, and for his . . . And they would all start singing.

"It's an eerie feeling, you know, when you see that, all of them singing and saluting, each individual before he goes to the chamber—I don't know how to explain it. It's a funny feeling. The song is very soft and sad, like: 'You are going to your death.' I saw that, standing on the side. It's—inside, it tightens you up. And, uh, you can say, 'This is war, you can't help it. Both sides are doing things. You can't help it.' You can think: 'Well, that's it,' but, uh . . .

"You have to be there, and see it, and hear it. It's not a nice feeling. It's sad."

—Eighty-year-old Japanese American man

|

# PROMISES

|

*THE SONG IS VERY SOFT and sad,* the man's voice says. *Inside . . .
it tightens you up.* The voice is past, taped in Tokyo on that
afternoon when Ian could not reach me. *Please don't use my
name. I have nothing special to say anyway.*

If it still seems that I can no longer write, at least I can
transcribe what I have gathered. This man was a Japanese
American, an "enemy alien" in Tokyo who was visited often
by the secret police, who was hired, at the end of the war,
by the Americans to help with the War Crimes interroga-
tions in Shanghai. He was a translator, probing for instances
of torture, of slaughter and rape, of following orders. Was
it justice? I asked him then, and neither of us knew the
answer. The tribunals were a gesture, no more than a sam-
pling, because, isn't war atrocious? When you're facing
down the enemy—when you both think you are right, and
the other is wrong—where can fairness come from? Where
is humanity?

In the absence of new interviews, the old ones whisper.
The Colonel proclaiming himself a hero; the young boy
giving a heroes' welcome to empty boxes of remains. I am
unlocking their voices in my room, playing their tapes, my
earphones muffling the sound of the boys jumping on the
futon. I am plugged into the past, scanning the tapes for
purpose. For a pitch to make to Brian that he won't reject.

Lily Onofrio is coming; I have just received an email

confirming that next week Lily will be visiting Japan. I have been waiting for months, hoping to meet her; I've been reading everything I can find about her story, and there are many questions I want to ask. This is the one interview I need and now, in this untouchable time, she is coming at last—coming to Fukuyama to visit her brother, and she will speak to me there.

This pitch sounds rushed and overly logical, even to me. Ami has gotten a television crew interested in the story. Maybe I do not want this coverage; maybe the crew will only get in the way. TV could make it explainable, though. Even inevitable. But how can it feel inevitable when I have never broached the subject once?

When the bomb drops, our lives must change: utterly, and forever. The only question is, will we look up or not? Will we recognize that moment when it happens, or only long after it has past? Will there be many moments—a procession, a spiral, a cloud—or only one, one we will live over and over again, until we can feel the world we knew slip out from under our feet and a new one come up to catch us, for good or bad, before we fall?

Here is the truth: I don't want to have to stay home to be loved. I don't want to believe I am loveable only as I was. If this is what we have come to, I will not let it stand unspoken. I will not say no to myself any longer, and I can only pray Brian will not say no to me.

I know that the promise I'm about to break is one that *I* made, an offering, unasked for. If this is true, it should be simple enough to change my mind. My lingering fear is that

I promised because Brian *was* asking, that it is a test—them or me—that I am about to fail.

I am going to Fukuyama to see Lily. There are no excuses anymore—no optimistic twisting. Jane's sister is dead. One of the other women I wanted to base my story on is dead too. But Lily is coming, Lily who may be one of the few people left alive who knows both the camps and the ruins of Hiroshima; one of the few people I can talk to who has not forgotten.

She has something to tell me that I need to know.

## BREATHING

**BREATHE.**

Breathe in, breathe out. Breathe again.

I am past the point of caring whether I am crying, whether I am yelling, whether Brian is pounding his chest with such fury and desperation that I imagine his sternum might actually break. Neither one of us can hold it down when the children are asleep or hold it back until the children are gone. I am beginning to experience sobbing the way a sick person experiences vomiting. I feel it coming; I fight against it; I do not want under any circumstances to give into it and lose control.

And yet, when I have lost my mind to my tears, lost any

concern for presentation, any ability to move or to censor what I'm saying, I am liberated. It is truthful, and animal, and when it's over, I am empty.

## ASK

WHEN THE CHILDREN are finally, possibly asleep, I leave. Do I say where? Would he believe me? Do we talk at all in these days, except to the children or in their presence, when they begin to cling to one or the other of us—sometimes even me now, but only out of fear, I suspect, since I am the one who left. I have taken Kimiko's old rusty mama-san out for a ride in the December evening, in my two layers of clothing and the men's jacket I bought at the Gap in the Shareo because nothing in the women's section fit me. My nose is running and freezing at the same time as I pedal faster to keep myself warm. When I'm tired, I will look for a set of stairs tucked near a bridge, the kind I like to hide in when I sit beside the river, sheltered from the wind.

Two nights ago, it was cold in our apartment, the heater set up in the bedroom for the children, so Brian and I sat at the *kotatsu* that Kimiko lent us for warmth, our lower bodies beneath the blanket at the table in the main room, and I made tea. That is where I finally told him about Lily, that I needed to travel to Fukuyama to do one last interview.

That is where his hands flew up and he came to his feet in a gesture that seemed born in the moment he first saw me in Narita airport. Where his words still linger in the broken air: "That's it. Do what you want from now on. I'm going back to New York."

There is no moon tonight along the river. The sky is clouded, so it's not so cold. I have dropped my bike in the grass and made my way to the set of stairs where I watched the paper lanterns launch from the landing at the Peace Park. How long ago that seems. It's dark here, but no one will bother me. The stone wall that doubles as the arch of the T-bridge is cold, and rough against my head. There's nothing here to keep me from my thoughts.

Brian's expression was as appalled as mine when he heard his own threat. His words unimagined by both of us. We left them there, both of us hoping he would not enact them, both of us knowing these were not idle words. If I had worried about my own responsibility for the slow dis-integration of our marriage, it never occurred to me that he would end it. That he could, simply, end it.

"Where is Fukuyama?" he asked. It was the beginning of an offer to follow me there, a willingness to backpedal; we could carry our struggle with us, draw it out without end. I heard his voice echoing off the walls of old conversa-tions: *The boys will be bored while you are working.*

"You don't want to come," I said.

"You don't want us to."

I could feel how it would go—Brian and the boys on the train. Me sitting with Lily while Brian waits somewhere nearby, hanging over me, a deadline, the exact pressure of being late to meet someone who is waiting on a busy corner. Could I invite them to Lily's brother's house? Send them to a castle, but who knew how long that would take? Interviews were just not a series of questions, they were experiences I wanted to think about afterward, mirrors I wanted to look into, thoughts to record in my notebooks for days. If Brian came too, impatiently waiting, wherever I settled him, for "it to be over," I would have to rush to put Lily away.

*You won't let us come because you don't know how long it will take? That's bullshit.*

I can no longer say what I'm doing. Not what I'm really doing, not even what I think I'm doing. I had no answer for him that night, only the stubborn truth that I did not want him there.

Brian says I'm a wreck. That I have fallen apart. That I have taken myself apart, disassembled who I was and left everything on the floor, where it spins and kicks but is no longer working. I am not the childhood sweetheart he married, I am no one he recognizes. I have forgotten who I was at home, and before that, who I was pre-children, and before that even, I forgot my very childhood.

But if I have a different view, that there was no mold for me in Japan so I've grown as I needed to, he is firm in his opinion that I should have definition, that we should both know who I am.

Who am I?

My mother knows. She always did, and that was my safety. That I existed in her, entire, even when I could not

290

put a name to myself or face the emotions and impulses inside me. Now I cannot seem to stop them from taking me over, but she is still the only one who can tell me what I should do now.

I could ask her.

*Come back to me.*

By the river where I watched the paper lanterns, the only light is from the cars that pass like ghosts on a mission. I close my eyes, waiting to feel my mother beside me. If there is a world of spirits, then surely we are also them incarnate, and we can call them to us.

*Who should I be?*

At one time in my life, I was embedded in my mother. In her knowing, and seeing, before I was consciously able to project what I thought I was. Before I was old enough to get mixed up in that projection, she knew me. What did she say to assure me? What words did she use, even when I was an adult, on the subway train, about to have a breakdown; how did she tell me *you are my child*? And if she is the only one who might still recognize me, is it me who is already gone?

*Who were you?*

There is no answer. When was the last time I felt my mother's presence? What was the last thing she said to me before my family arrived? It is crazy to me that I cannot remember this. I was given a gift, to know her, how could I have let that slip away, not have cherished those revelations? They are written somewhere, in my diary in the house where Brian waits, but how can they not exist in my mind? My mother was always there for me. I remember her body lying next to mine, holding me on the day when I was five and I stole bubblegum from the local store. I remember the orchid she put on a plate next to my sandwich when she was the only one I allowed in my room on those first, postpartum depression days after Ian was born. Where did she get an orchid in Brooklyn? How did she wear her hair in those days?

What did she say to me that day, on my bed, or did she say nothing?

*Talk to me.*

Where did you go? How can you have left me? I am not ready for this, not equipped yet—I know I should be, a thirty-seven-year-old woman and a mother in my own right, but you are the one who made me a mother, you are the one who said, *things will change.* What do I do now, that they are changing? What do I do with the boys who will not hug me for more than an instant, who send their cheerful I love yous from across the room? What do I give up for them? And what of this husband of mine who will not love me as I am, who will not let me love him, who wants the life he had, the wife he had, and feels cheated that these were not objects, immutable and possessable? He wants to know who I intend to be now; he wants me to propose it so we can negotiate who I will be.

*Help me. Please.*

The night is dark, and me the only presence. Maybe all these visitations were nothing after all, figments and fractures in my memory. There will come a time when my mother will no longer recognize me, when I will sit beside her bed, holding her hand. Will it matter if I'm there if she doesn't know me? Or might it not matter who you are as long as you are there? Whose memory is important then, which identity?

My mother is standing in her darkened hallway, but now I can go to her. For this, I need only to feel. When I gather her in my arms, both of us are the same size, both of us shaking; I can whisper to her as she once did to comfort me. Is it her, or me, I am afraid of losing? Is it her last moment of perfect understanding that I'm afraid is already past us, or my own? I didn't get to say how much I loved her—not then, in her tears, not when I could have summed it all up, given it force, pulled together every beat of my heart and given it back to her.

But I can hold her now, hold myself, our hands a lifeline that cannot be broken. I will keep her with me, long after she's gone, because how can I survive without her?

## LILY

SHE LOOKS LOST in the train station lobby, standing just past the turnstiles, rotating her entire body as if she cannot begin to decide where she should settle herself while she waits. Japanese women are small, but this one could not weigh more than ninety pounds. She cocks her head as I approach and turns again: a wry smile, a stiff neck from the airplane, a strong embrace for a stranger. And then, birdlike, her shoulders tight and careful, she indicates that I should follow her.

"Reiko-chan," she says. That smile. Those great big eyes, broad cheekbones. "How do you like Japan?"

We will spend all day together, Lily and I. She will be passionate and bossy, and will speak in a voice too soft for my tape recorder. She knows I have read her story, read it in an anthology before I met her and then read everything she sent me in the box on her experience at Tule Lake. She knows I'm not interested in that part of her life as much as what happened after, but life is life, and that is where her story begins.

THERE IS A CAMP in the California desert where the enemy aliens are being held. Nine thousand agitators, disloyals, identified, rounded up, shipped out, held without legal status, or benefit of the Geneva Convention, for the good, the safety, of our country. Nine thousand grandparents, babies, young women dying in childbirth because there's no medical care in the camp.

This is not the kinder, gentler camps of my own family's stories. The stakes are higher here. The world is darker.

This is Tule Lake.

Here is a father who said, *You took away our rights, our citizenship, our homes, and now we feel justified to say "no" when you try to draft us into your army.* Here is a young man, a seventeen-year-old brother, who, for no more reason than

294

that refusal to be drafted, is pulled out of bed in a dragnet, placed in the "bullpen," left for days without food or shelter, beaten with bats, sticks, and rifles, leaving skin and matted hair and blood for the Caucasian women to clean up. He is left for a year in the "stockade," he and hundreds of others, despite international protests from the Spanish consulate and the ACLU.

Picture a young woman, pregnant. She has two children, ages five and seven, and she's just been released from the hospital after a tumor operation. American citizen, law-abiding. Take away her husband, kill off her mother-in-law. Hound her with illness, allergies, food poisoning, premature labor; give her new, five-pound infant double pneumonia. Deport her to Hiroshima, to the rubble where her father was killed by the atomic bomb and her mother was burned and hairless and very slowly dying. Pull her children away, in body and mind, so that in her older age, they do not speak.

"People always ask me about Tule Lake."

TELL ME.

I want to hear about the transport ship that brought her back to Japan. I want to hear about the road home, the time spent in Hiroshima after the war. What was it like to find her mother in the ruins of the city, to be cast out by her own family when she arrived? I want to know how Lily survived, with so many lives imploding around her: her brother's friends, her own, committing suicide because, how does one face these days, of betrayal, of no hope? I want to know how long it took her to return to the US, how she finally regained her citizenship, how tortuous that route, and why she would bother after what America did to her. This was my original question for her: What do you do when you are rejected by two countries? How do you choose who to be? There is something else now, something briefly mentioned in her published story, that has taken on a sudden urgency: What happened, exactly, with her husband?

"At the time [when she returned to Hiroshima], my husband was in Nagasaki, and I guess he had already started a family or was living with someone else."

THIS IS WHAT I KNOW of Lily's story. It was her husband who asked to be "repatriated" to Japan, along with his parents, so she agreed to go along. After that, he was sent to a justice department camp, much like a prisoner of war camp, and although they exchanged a few highly censored letters, she never saw him again.

She had agreed to go to Japan with them, but she was ill. Her youngest child barely surviving. Lily's mother-in-law died in the camps, afraid and screaming; she was carried, ashes in a box, strapped to Lily's father-in-law's chest until he too was taken, and Lily was alone. Then, without her own family, without her husband's, she changed her mind.

Did her husband know that she would have refused to leave if she could have? After he and her father-in-law were moved to the other camp, Lily tried everything she could to stay in the country where she was born, but in the end, her country forced her to go. And when she and her three children arrived in the ruins, after three years of separation, her husband was there and had already remarried.

Did they lose each other in the letters? Did they lose each other because of time? Was it the choices they had to make in different worlds, with no bridge between them? Lily was caught in a war; she lost her family in a war, fighting all the way without any idea of how to fight, or whom. Was it pain suffered, isolating, that was the final straw? Could it have been so simple?

*Tell me what happened to you.*

"Oh, Reiko," Lily tells me now after she has shared so many memories, "things happen. And that's life." You can fight, she says, and oh, she was a fighter!, but hoping the world will be any different is useless. It just makes things worse.

"I learned that the hard way."

Lily smiles again—wry, twisted. She is eighty-five years old.

"You have to get away," she says. "Move on. Of course, you have to do your best, do everything you can do, but in the end, you can't change the world. Right? You can't even change your husband!" She laughs. We are standing. Going now to meet her brother. "He left. After everything. So what is that? What is fair?"

"We were sent to Japan on a transport ship, me and my children; it was a hospital ship full of sick people. I didn't want to go, but they refused to let me stay. They said: 'You have no employable skills; you have no one to take you. To guarantee that you would have a home for yourself and your children. You would become a public charge.'

"The US government would not keep anyone who would be a public charge. They had already taken away my citizenship, so I needed a sponsor, and even though I had a brother in the US Army, working as a translator, they would not allow him to sponsor us.

"When we arrived in Japan, they dumped us in the ocean. There was no pier, no shore. There was a small boat brought to the shore and we had to wade in the water up to here . . . We were put with a group of Japanese soldiers who had just been released from the Philippines—all ragged clothes, ragged everything, ready to tackle me. They stole everything. Because they didn't have any clothes, any shoes. They were dumped, like we were dumped. We had nothing to eat, but my brother— the soldier brother—had given us some hard things, hard cookies. But we didn't have time to eat them because the soldiers came and stole . . . they stole our blankets and then I started menstruating, and there was no paper and we were exposed . . . My kids cried, especially my youngest daughter who was born in the camp, they were saying, 'Let's go back to America.'

"You know, looking back at how America thought, I can see them deciding that we adults could fend for ourselves. But I had three small children who were all American citizens, and I thought—they deserved to stay."

—Lily Onofrio

THE DAYS ARE SHORTER now. The time between sunrise and sunset, my time in Japan—it's getting harder to see the road, harder to know where we're going. We wake up in the morning and move, packing the silence between us, sightseeing to save the marriage. Brian and I are living in a truce of exhaustion: it is undeclared; it is as soft as sorrow, and as lonely. I can feel the divide between us, our responses to the same experience sliding to the opposite ends of the scale, one A, one Z, and I can't help but wonder if the scale we used has always been rigged, bowed to the middle, and what was once a cupped parabola sliding us into a tangled heap at its vertex is now upside down—a cruel joke with no common resting place except for one spot of impossible twinship. We are crossing through a plateau: every kind gesture is too slight for true pleasure; every frustration expected and overlooked. We are too tired for reaction, and leery of the time when we are not.

And what's more, we are coming up on Christmas, wending our way through mountain roads in the snow and the night in a rented car with a map marked only in kanji. *Zutto massugu, soshite ni-ban me o migi* with some hand signals can usually get us where we're going, although once, we were so lost in a valley that I leaped into the road to flag down the only passing car we'd seen in twenty minutes, and the driver obligingly led us poor foreigners through the mountains to the highway, then turned around and continued on his own way.

Our way, on this last sightseeing tour of Japan, is to Hagi and Tsuwano, two historic castle towns northwest of Hiroshima, both of which have been recommended by friends as "little Kyotos." Our only companions on this white day in Tsuwano are the fat carp in the canals on either side of the main street that barely bother to twitch at the specially purchased carp food we're dropping on their heads, and, earlier this morning when we climbed to the top of the hill to the Taikodani Inari shrine, our footprints in the snow. We were the first pilgrims on this walk, the winding path up the hill to the shrine bridged by one thousand red toriis so close, in certain places, that the gates function as a tunnel not even the falling snow can penetrate. The quiet was profound, and more resounding than Dylan and Ian, based as it was on the red and white of our walk, the black and white of the samurai quarters below us, the green and white of the forest that eats its slow way into the castle ruins on the next hill. Besides the shrine and the husk of the castle, Tsuwano has temples, museums, paper artisans, steam locomotives, and even a Catholic church. What it lacks is public toilets.

"Finding a potty" has become a family obsession, and something of a conundrum since New York has no public bathrooms, while Japan's are usually plentiful, clean, and furnished with at least one Western toilet (reliably found at the far end of the row) plus a vending machine for packets of tissue. It seems like a misprint, a problem with the storyteller, that our lives circle back on these bodily functions. So

301

when Ian "has to go" just as lunch arrives at our table at the small *udon-ya* that has no bathroom, gratitude oozes over my wet, tired shoulders when Brian stands up to take him. The proprietor points them to the train station just across the street. As Brian and Ian re-layer their sweaters, Dylan and I settle into our seats, taking in the wooden beams, the scruffy workmen on their lunch break, the simple painted bowls. He is merely happy to see noodles, and to drain his full glass of soda, while I find myself released to say yet another small goodbye in the series of leave-takings my life has become. I set my nose over the rich, plentiful heap of melting "mountain vegetables" in my soup, drawing it into me before it cools enough to eat, cradling the nutty, sour, slippery mouthfuls of tubers and greens I have come to love and may never taste again.

Dylan insisted he didn't have to go to the bathroom with Brian and Ian, and, of course, minutes after they return, he changes his mind. I weigh his announcement against the seven minutes of udon that remain in my bowl and decide he can finish his food first. He wiggles. I notice, and wonder if it's a bad idea.

This is a meal—that's all it is: one meal I would love to eat from first to last bite uninterrupted. This is a test: if I can have this, maybe I can go back to who I was. I can be a mother. I have become stuck on this: the woman Brian wants is a mother, a member of his united, happy family, not a person who might be called away to do her job and may or may not come home for dinner. If this is simplistic, if this is flat out wrong, still, these are the labels I'm using to grapple with the struggle between us. I believe that if I can agree to be this mother, my marriage and my family will be saved.

This is my focus as I pretend to ignore Dylan's fidgeting, until I realize he has moved from not-at-all-interested-in-the-potty to not-at-all-interested-in-his-food. My test failed. My next two minutes would probably be better spent getting him into his coat and through one hundred yards of snow.

We dress and leave Brian to finish up and pay the bill.

The wind has picked up and is slanting the snow into my collar. I shove Dylan's hat on his head and we dash hand in hand across the empty street to the public restroom beside the train station. It is equally vacant.

A ghost town in the snow.

"*Mom! Mom!* I have to go *now*!"

"I know, Dylan. Just . . . " I am checking the stalls, only to find that there are no Western toilets. Which would be okay, except the floors are unusually puddled and there are no vending machines for toilet paper.

"*Mom!*"

I know he has to go. He is dancing, and I'm trying to pick the cleanest option. Japanese toilets are ceramic basins set into the floor, shaped more like a rectangle than an oval, but just a bit too wide for a small boy in blue jeans to straddle. Peeing is no problem, but that is not, apparently, what Dylan needs to do, which means he's going to have to take one oversized hiking shoe off, slip one leg out of his pants and put his foot back into the shoe without getting his sock soaked in the puddles on the floor, which would be difficult to start with, but will be impossible with this dance. I have tissues in my pocket, but not enough to swab the floor first, and no real inclination to do so. It's likely that the mess is melted snow, but I don't know.

This is who I'm supposed to be. I am taking a breath.

"Mom, now! *Now!*"

I look into his face, screwed tight as it is with need, and am torn between pity and a suffocating anger: why in the hell didn't my poor, sweet child give me just a little more warning? I throw open the door to the closest stall and step in, no longer caring about cleanliness; if he gets dirty, it's his fault for not going with Brian. My attention is downward to avoid the puddles and not on the wall in front of me in case there is, oh, a shelf sticking off it, so when my forehead slams into this protrusion, the stars that shoot into the back of my head with the pain are actually frightening. I have been ambushed, and I am screaming "Shit!" and rearing backward and into the door that has not closed completely, but is stuck on Dylan so that it rams straight into the back of my head at the only angle that has absolutely no perpendicular force to deflect it. Now, the words coming out of my mouth are even more inappropriate for small children. Dylan is crying because he really has to go and I can barely see because the pain from both sides of my head is sending rip tides into my ears, and oh how I want to be a child again myself, I want someone to get me out of there, out of this atmosphere I can't breathe in and this bathroom that is attacking me still. I know I have to help Dylan—I cannot do it, I am incapable of pulling his pants down, and yet, somehow, I do.

He tries to straddle. He can't straddle. He wants to take his pants off so he can get one leg on each side of the floor basin and he is still crying.

Actually removing his pants will be the end of me. "It's okay, Dylan. It's okay. Do you have to pee?"

"No."

"Are you *sure* you don't have to pee?"

"No. I mean yes. I mean, no I don't have to pee."

"Okay, so, we'll face this way." I steer him so that he's squatting with his back toward the potty, butt hanging over the basin, American style, with his pants around his ankles. "Don't worry about your pants. It's no problem."

"But *Mom* . . . "

He knows this is the wrong way to face on a Japanese potty, and my three-year-old wants so much to do everything correctly.

"Don't worry Dylan. Just don't pee."

"But . . . "

Hobbled, he has nothing to hold onto to keep him up, so I move in front of him and slightly to one side so he can brace himself on my arm. When he is set, holding the length of my forearm like a water skier, it turns out that he has to pee, which he does in an arch over his bunched-up pants and within inches of mine. It's impossible to make him stop, or point him in the right direction. It is spraying all over the floor, all over the wall of the stall. If he keeps the stream high, we, at least, might escape without getting soaked, but I cannot direct him to do this; he is using both hands to keep himself from falling and I can do nothing to save us from my folly at the last minute, because it is clear—oh, how clear—that this is my fault, my selfishness that he's suffering, and there's no longer anything I can do.

He is still sniffling; I'm assuring him that it's okay, not his fault, we will both dry; and my forehead is still on fire. I am replaying all my failures as a mother, and I remember, suddenly, the first time I ever hit one of my children—it was Ian, he was two, and for those first two years he was my angel and I had protected him fiercely. And then Dylan was born, a plump, squalling baby who cried all night and ate all day. And one day, when Dylan was breastfeeding, my angel walked over and bit Dylan's face in mid-suck—and I shoved Ian to the floor. Hard, without even thinking about it, I hurt one child I loved to protect the other. It was appalling, but the worst part was, I didn't process it, consider it, decide—I just struck. I am appalled now, even more appalled because this time there's no backhanded excuse of maternal instinct. There's no forgiveness in the fact that Dylan managed to miss us both with his urine. My child is dissolving because of me, because I could not see him or make room for his needs, and all I can do now is to wipe his bottom, and then, in penance, use the rest of the tissues to clean the floor and the wall he aimed at.

*Shhh . . . It's okay. It's okay, Dylan.*

Then, when he is zipped and straightened and I have blown his nose, I scoop my baby into my arms and hug him. He hugs me back—a tight pulse of love and relief that lasts past the point when we have righted ourselves and flows into the warmth of safety. I can feel him, who he is: his concerns, his worries, his needs, curiosities, and preoccupations. I know him; I have always known him. *He is my child.* There is a union—not a link between abstractions, but a world of color and light and love between my sorry, uncertain self and this small person in my arms. It's the same feeling I had when I first fell in love with Ian: that he was a real, distinct individual. Mysterious, ever-changing, I can feel his essence: everything he will be already existing; a mind, a heart, a soul in this pudgy body waiting to be seen.

I lost my children. Or perhaps I never had them. He is clutching me as if he can sink into me, pull his body through my skin. Is this the first time I've felt this in him, this fierce and utter love? I am standing for both of us, holding us up, but he is saving me.

I love my children. Oh, how I want them.

Dylan settles against me, still hugging, but no longer clinging. I keep him circled in one arm and put the other hand on his heart. I can feel the beating in my palm, the heart that is open, will open to me despite everything I've done. I want to give him what my mother gave me, that security of being known, the comfort of presence. I cannot hold him still for my convenience—I have to let him grow, take on new forms, change direction. Which is exactly what I have to do for my mother: accept her the way she is.

When he has finally had enough, Dylan releases me and pulls just slightly away, pushing the hair off my forehead to get a closer look at the purple egg that has appeared there.

"Oooh . . . That's a good one!"

I know. I can feel it—still in my ears and also under my

fingertips—it must be standing an inch off my head. Was it a shelf? A peg? I can't remember what the stall looked like, but I'm going to carry this one for a long time.

When we step outside, Brian is waiting. The car is running in the parking lot near the door, puffing steam out the exhaust. The snow is falling in fat, horizontal flakes, wrapping the muffler of silence around them again: warm, secure, restored. When I put Dylan in his car seat, he proudly lifts my hair to show his father the bruise on my forehead.

"Look, Dad."

"Christ. What in the hell happened to you?"

I look at Brian, and my sons, and the falling snow, and I have no idea how to answer.

|

## MOSHI MOSHI

|

WHEN I CALL TO WISH THEM a merry Christmas, my father answers, like he always does.

"It's your daughter," he calls out, settling my mother on the receiver and then dashing to get the other extension. I can hear her breathing, waiting for the phone to speak.

"*Moshi moshi*," I greet her.

"*Moshi moshi*," she replies, "*moshi mosh*." This is what my mother has said to me on the telephone all my life, what my grandmother used to say. I take comfort in the fact that she still remembers this, still seems to recognize my voice, so much like hers that other people cannot tell us apart, though I cannot overlook how deft my father has become at announcing who is on the phone. And then, "Where are you?"

I tell her I am still in Japan. She says, "Oh, no wonder you're not home." She asks what I am up to.

We are traveling, I tell her. I describe Tsuwano, with its carp-filled moats; the black and white castle town of Hagi, where we searched for their signature pottery. I try to make her laugh with a story about the boys and their Japanese words. They love it here, love the food, the fish-shaped *manju* filled with chocolate custard. I remember, when I left New York, each of my sons put together a book of photographs of himself for me to look at. When I showed them to friends, their comment on my baby was "*Itsumo tabeta.*" And they were right; in every picture, he was eating. I recall this story for her, tell her about Brian's dried fish breakfasts, and how the boys like to challenge him to eat the most dubious-looking things. When I have finished my update, have made her laugh, I ask my parents, "So, what's new with you?"

They have just celebrated Christmas, but my father doesn't say anything for a moment. This is how he measures my mother: he is waiting for her to speak. Finally, he prompts her. "What's new here?" he says.

"Oh . . . " she says, gaily. "We're boring. What's new with you?"

And so I tell her again, from the beginning. My father listens without comment as I add some new details—how the

309

carp didn't even flinch when the food we dropped on them hit the tops of their impassive heads. I add "I might have told you" casually to what I've already said in case my answer suddenly seems familiar: it's important that she doesn't suspect, that she doesn't get depressed. I start again with Tsuwano and its carp-filled moats, then move on to the black and white castle town of Hagi. It is not until she begins to laugh in the same places, that I can relax into it, knowing I will tell her a third time if she repeats her question.

I am talking to my mother; she is listening. And, in this moment, I will cherish every word.


|

## COURT MUSIC

|


I WAKE TO THE ALARM: a nameless, repeating dirge played by the bastard child of an electric keyboard and a kazoo, the world-time clock which I set only once before the family arrived, in the pre-dawn of August sixth. Brian's back is curved away from me as I lie down again and try to pull my way out of sleep. Today marks fourteen years of marriage and a preceding seven of life together: it's our wedding anniversary.

*The bugaku is performed in only three places in Japan, and one of them is Miyajima. It's the New Year and . . .* This is what I'd hoped to give him: the wail of the *shō*; the simple

repetition of the traditional court dance; the dragging brocade costumes. It was an omen that the program I'd longed
to see for most of my stay in Japan was to be performed on
the day we were married, a day that once was perfect, and
in one of the three most beautiful places in Japan. Today
was going to be our new start: 2002, a morning when we
planned to wake before the sunrise, when we planned to
erase. When we thought we could turn to each other as
strangers, unhurt, not rejected; when we could rekindle the
excitement of meeting for the first time.

But there are things we cannot let go of.

Last night, in those hours before this chapter could be
forever closed, when we might have been able to file this
away with all the wrong labels—yes, I am a mother; yes,
I am going home—we finally hit the wall. With the anger
banished, and a bottle of sake to accompany us, we sat in our
bedroom on the tatami and looked out onto the river. The
street lights were enough to see by, as much as we wanted to
see. Surrounded by the life I had chosen—just a floor, sliding paper doors, futons spread out to sleep on—he found
the heart of his sorrows.

"You never wanted to come home," he said into the darkness. "You should have missed our life together, but you
didn't. I waited for you, but you didn't want to come home."

In his voice, a child lost. I felt for my own responses.
Excuses came first, a way out, words I could attack to
rewrite this verdict he had issued. *You didn't ask. You could
have come here. You were so angry all the time* . . . But I knew
these weren't fair and would not save us.

There will come a time when I will describe it this way: that in that moment I realized I had become intimate with war. Once, I had asked about the effect of war on the individual lives of people: *And what about war? Not, who fights, or who dies, or how does the amputated family rise from the ashes, but how does it change the people we are?* In Brian's voice, I could hear how war can be measured: the collective consequence of where we stood, what shielding we had from the blast. Whether we fled.

I fled. I was afraid of losing myself, of losing my family, of the turmoil and helplessness of war, so I held off the pain beneath Brian's anger; I held him to his promises and judged him for being unable to fulfill them. I experienced him as a bully: he was the one who defined and categorized, and I offered no alternative interpretations. And if I felt rejected, he too felt abandoned.

Both of us, tipping and trapped. Both of us reacting to the velocity of the trigger.

IT IS SNOWING when we leave the apartment, but by the time we reach Miyajima, the temperature has dropped, clearing all but a sifting of white from the sky. It is my coldest day in Japan. We disembark from the ferry: first stop is the bathroom, then to pet the deer. *Don't be scared, just don't touch its antlers, see the stumps where they cut them off? You can feed the little ones. It's okay. Take your time.* Time is the key to our day; we pretend we have a lot of it.

We walk, with great deliberation, down the middle of the gamut of "any things" for sale. The streets between the pier and the famous Itsukushima Shrine are lined with post-cards, painted fans, key chains, and plastic trucks. Wooden *shakushi* of every size painted with various kanji; wooden bowls; wooden plates. Oyster bars with windows display-ing lengths of shell-encrusted ropes from the Seto Inland Sea; open barbeques with fresh oysters on the grill. And, of course, the ubiquitous *momiji manju,* the maple leaf-shaped sponge cakes filled with red bean paste that are the specialty of the island. We watch the assembly-line machines pour the batter, scoop the filling, and bake them before our eyes. And we stop—today being what it is; my boys being crea-tures who need fuel, who look on anything sweet, not as a taste, but as something to be consumed in multiples. These will hold us while we walk through the arcade, still strolling for the shrine.

I am trying not to get caught in the aimless currents of shopping. Even if there's no hurry, even if I'm moving as if my space boots are all that keep me from floating away, I have pinned my future on this performance. It's a symbol of what I've given my old life up for, and a gauge of what I'm moving toward. This is my boys' first chance to step onto the wooden walkway of the shrine that floods when it storms; their first wild shake of the white paper wands over their heads to cleanse themselves at the shrine entrance. We are here at last, but the stages are empty. The boys drag Brian toward the narrow pier that fronts the shrine and point to the floating torii—they have found open ground, and they each have a hand—and their momentum allows me to wave them off and see if I can find out what's going on.

313

The boys are beginning to flip over the low railing that encloses the stage. Three *shimai* performances are scheduled before the *bugaku* we have come for; each is a half an hour long. These dances are simple—there are no masks or elaborate costumes—and the stage is placed right in the middle of a milling crowd in a tent, and so, even though many people stop to see what's going on, they aren't exactly rapt. Attention is good for five minutes, and then, since the small gaijin boys cannot drift toward the sake with the others, they twist and whine and wiggle and talk.

I could shush them, make them watch. I could measure the distance between how bored they are and how much I would love this with any one of the Japanese friends I have made here, and use it as proof that I can't be a mother, but today, I will not. Three performances is long enough to do something else before the *bugaku*, and on this island, not too far from here, is the temple where I went firewalking. I stoop to pull them to me, hold them still and close to me on either side as I tell them about the long steps, the room of *jizo*s at the top, and the ceremony of fire. *You walked on fire, on the flames? And you weren't burned, really?* They are captivated, ready to race ahead and then they do, checking back at every branch in the path, leaving Brian and me to walk together. He is sad and settled; I don't know what he's thinking. I've lived here long enough to know that an answer is not correct just because it is timely, so I don't press him. Bad news comes when it comes.

"You should do what you want from now on," he told

me last night. "Finish your interviews. Your time here is your own."

All this time, I was waiting for love to save us. I was waiting for the truth to present itself, for the happy ending. *You never wanted to come home*, he'd said, and it seemed important to let that stand. It was true. I have to own that. I have to feel it, because it is how he feels. He had something that disappeared, and who am I to say that he shouldn't want it? It was his, was what he loved, and he was who he was because of it. We all have the right to imagine ourselves as we want to be, and to try to make that real.

There will come another night when we will write our own metaphor. It will be summertime, in New York, after months of him asking for parameters and definitions, and me not being able to say. We built a treehouse, he will say to me, and it was perfect. And I will imagine a boat, one that could take us anywhere; I will describe it, and how we could build it, and I will ask him to join me in it.

*But I like the treehouse.* I can still hear his voice. *I want the treehouse.*

For some reason, I will place this exchange on our futon, in our room as it was last night, as we looked out over the river. That's how memory is: imperfect. That's how the future embeds in the past. But it may also be that I place it here because last night, I made a decision. Though he did not leave Japan early as he threatened to, I will stay here after he leaves. There's an end I haven't reached yet. I will postpone my trip home for another two weeks.

He is leaving me. In my head, I try out this configuration of words. They sound strange but just as right as the switch of the pronouns: I am leaving him.

Is this how divorce happens? I wonder. You wake up to a day when pronouns do not matter? When it's no longer surprising that the one you loved doesn't want you anymore?

Right now, today, I am still surprised. There will be plenty of time ahead to become used to the idea. I will try until I cannot anymore because that is who I am, and he will never be the one who would step out the door, which has always been him. The death of a marriage is a long course toward exhaustion. The last breath may not even be remembered.

The boys are ahead of us, stopped on a long promenade of steps lined on either side with engraved stone pickets that record the donations to the temple. They have been worried about their parents, linking us in a chain for most of the day as if they knew we were about to fly apart, but this place has liberated them. First they crouch down beside the tiny statues, then spin gold through their fingers as they zigzag up the stairs. Now they are reading kanji. Just a few. They are checking each donation marker—there are hundreds on each side—for my name, the "Mommy character," an older and uncommon kanji; they are looking for *ko*, which means child; for *kawa*, the three lines that look like a river; *ta* the box with the cross through it that signals a rice field. They are looking for themselves in Japan: Ian methodical in his search; Dylan running up and down the walk, racing backward, leaping, always about to fall. This is a day, that's all it is; it doesn't have to be an omen. It doesn't have to be the end of something, or the first sign of what's to come.

WE ARE SITTING on a bench in the cold, eating fried and frittered food. Our visit to the temple has restored us somewhat, and the plentitude of French fries seems to be finishing the job. Dylan is entirely focused on his chicken fingers and I'm enjoying my octopus balls; we've each chosen what we wanted, and our delight in finding it overshadows the fragile fact that our choices are entirely different. This small allowance in the seams of our life allows us to breathe, so when the snow begins to fall again and Brian spots a crowd gathering around the stage at the shrine behind us, we leave our food behind and take off together. The music has begun, but the stage holds only snow, and there's a place for four in the front in the center as the bugaku begins.

There are four dancers on the small, raised platform. They're surrounded by a low, orange railing, flanked by the copper lanterns, backed by the smaller lantern and the *torii*. They are older, stern-looking men—not lithe or beautiful, not breathtaking in their movements. What they are is a perfect fit in their setting. Their costumes are principally green and gold and orange—in traditional Japanese fashion, they are multilayered, thick and cozy, the prints overlap and do not quite match, the final drape is diagonal so that their sleeves, when they bring them together, are different colors. Their robes have long trains and their shoes are odd and elfin; their hats are helmets of brocade and gold with knobs and points and curls and feathers. The shoes are simple fabric creations in white with a center seam and a silhouette that suggests leprechauns, or maybe the comb of a rooster. The music, of course, is eerie and sad and somewhat screeching and clashing, and it doesn't follow the dance, which is very simple and repetitive. The dance circles; arms sweep back and forth and hold; there is some stomping and heel work—it looks like a cross between hula, mime, and clogging.

It is otherworldly, and exactly what we came for.

There are only two dances. But I am standing with my family when my baby, my Daddy's boy who has not come to me once in Japan if his father was also an option, climbs into my arms. The trains on the dancers' robes are tracing tracks on the stage and the world beyond the torii has faded into white, much as the islands on the edge of the Seto Inland Sea drop out of view in the late day's haze, and the *shō* is lifting into the air, when my son pats my head with one hand and dangles the other down from his perch to hold my hand. In the empty space beside me, I imagine my mother beside us, just a memory of her, and I know that I will finish what I started here, that there is not only one, unyielding choice. Life is both, not one or the other. Not opposites. And there is something more—born of my new self or allowed because of it, or perhaps always there but never seen until I reached this perspective—my joy in encountering my children. As my fairytale marriage enters the woods, there are breadcrumbs: my trust in the small fingers that are melting the snow in my hair.

# |
# THE MAP
# |

HERE IS THE PRIEST with the map. Here are the yards of
paper I first encountered on my trip with Ami to her family's graveyard during Obon, and hundreds of photographs.
If Ami urged me to look at Japan in context, here is one: the
ruined past of the town that used to thrive on the point of
land directly under the hypocenter. Nakajima.

It was a bustling place, Toshiro Ogura tells me, his fingers wandering down the missing streets, pointing out buildings and landscape. In the Meiji and Taisho eras, there were
movie theaters, cafes, billiard saloons, and lots of shopping
on the main streets. It was a port: "Nakajima-cho" means
the town in the middle of an island. Lumber, rice, and other
crops were carried here by boat down the Otagawa. Also,
from the islands in the Seto Inland Sea, fruits and vegetables
arrived. Here, he shows me, the banks were lined with special steps that worked as wharfs. This is where the goods
arrived. It was a living town, a busy mercantile, and business center, full of wholesalers and retailers.

There were ten temples in the not-so-big town of
Nakajima.

This one, Joho-ji, near the bridge where the main street
curves, about ten meters from where the memorial cenotaph is now, was his father's.

*This is me,* he points out, going through the photographs,
*the sixteenth generation of my family. This is my family, and*

*this is me again . . . in thirteenth year of Showa (1938). This is Grandmother in front of the temple. This is Father, Mother, and this is my sister Reiko.*

In the rippling black and whites, the mother sits, the girl at her feet, her husband in Western clothes and a fedora. A family pose so familiar I feel I have seen these people before. Here, again, are the lily of the valley arches, the ladies in kimonos in better times. And over there, against the ubiquitous backdrop of wooden gates, a grandmother: small, and decorated, with careful hair. It is not that I know her. It's that I know this search through memory.

Ogura-san takes out another, newer map and points to the overlaps: the bridges that stand in both eras, the contours of the river banks; he superimposes the Peace Park, where the monuments hover over the past. He's concerned that the city wants to pull down the Rest House, the only building left standing in the park, so that it can put up something clean and modern. He's worried the government is trying to get rid of the few "dirty and old parts of the city" that are left. The old parts are our witness to the past, he says, and I understand. I've been in the basement of the Rest House, once a small kimono fabric store built in 1929, where almost no one goes. Above ground: the tourists and the brochures and the booth that will put your picture on stickers. Below: me in a hard hat, in a wet concrete ruin, where the shadow of Hiroshima lies.

Ogura-san is talking about the restoration. He's afraid that visitors to the Peace Park cannot feel what happened there, but instead are relieved that the hypocenter was quite near to a park so there were not many people affected. He is talking about now, about the future, but in the pictures he is flipping, the past is unrelenting. The family.

*This is me, the sixteenth generation of my family.*

He is the only survivor. Everyone in his family was killed. One hundred and seventy of the two hundred people in his father's parish also died. Almost no one in the bustling town of Nakajima survived. His context, then: he is an orphan. His fifteen-year-old sister, forced to make weapons parts in a munitions factory in Tenma-cho, was injured and suffered for a day before she died. He was bounced around between cousins while he was growing up. I think of Tokita-san and wonder why this man isn't filled with anger. *Looking back,* he says, off hand, *I have something I feel strange about. No one around me spoke ill of the United States.*

As if blame was too inconsequential for the vast emptiness that was there.

And sadness, too. In the newspaper articles I read about this man, the relative who finally came to get him after the war says he was a stoic boy who didn't cry when he heard the news of the deaths of his parents and his sister, but instead tried to comfort her. I ask him about this, but he doesn't remember what he was thinking. He remembers seeing Hiroshima again: *I was overwhelmed. I was shocked. I felt hollow, and looked around.* He struggled, he tells me that, and I think of him, a young boy, alone. Struggle is good, he says. Sometimes, you have to go on alone.

Ogura-san is not just remembering the bomb, he is using it, trying to anchor it by threading it through his life.

Tokita-san too. I wanted it to be tangible, and if it is not entire, not epic, the bomb still lives on in every deed they do. They are making peace, and it works better without anger, without blame. In thinking of myself in the Peace Museum, of Brian, of the US and its busy bombing, I understand how rare it is to heal.

And in the end, when the priest closes the map, when the photos are gone and we are drinking tea, I thank him. I apologize for taking his time, and for making him repeat his story, which must be so boring for him. He smiles and tells me that now is where the future lies. It is time again, chasing its tail. Time moves from present to past, Ami told me. He is telling me that the present—this instant—is everything, because in every moment, there's a possibility that something wonderful is about to happen:

*Ichi go, ichi e.*

*Each time we encounter another person in our lives,* he tells me, *it may be the last time, and it may be very important, something may happen in that moment to change both of our lives. Yes, I have done many interviews, but this time between us cannot be replaced. This is our time: just once, you and me.*

"Here is a photo of the ruins of my father's parish after the A-bomb. You can see that there are still tombstones in the graveyard. This is me, a high school student. I didn't know the parishioners' names, but I knew that, during Obon and in the New Year, people would come back and visit their ancestors' graves, so I put up a post and placed a glass bottle at the bottom of it. I put a note in the bottle asking people who visited the graves to write down their whereabouts. Gradually the news came, and I started to visit those families' homes.

"I had thought, ever since I could remember, that I should succeed to my father's temple, but I also knew I did not have sufficient mental training to be a priest. I didn't think I was worthy of being paid as a priest, on one hand, but I needed some economic support too, so I thought I would become a medical doctor. It was ideal: a doctor deals with the physical condition of people, and a priest deals with their mental condition. But it was too much work to do both, so I came back to the starting point. Which was, to be a priest. Now I think it was a good decision.

"In life, there are many elements you can choose, but there are others you cannot do anything about. When I found out that I was orphaned, I didn't like it. I thought it was not what I intended, and for some time my state of mind was unstable. There were moments I could have fallen away from a straight, just path. But gradually I realized that this was my life, that I could not exchange mine for any other person's. I have come to realize I have been supported by many people, and I owe my existence to them. Being an orphan was my background and backbone. If I had not lost my parents and I had led an easier life, I would not be the person I am now. I think of my past in a positive way.

"These days, I visit prisons in my role as a chaplain. I always tell people there that it is very good if you do not fall. But people are apt to trip. If you get up back on the right track, then the experience will enrich your life. If you don't get up, you reach the end, and you lose. But getting up is great."

—Toshiro Ogura

# WRITING

I'VE SPENT THE LAST seven months assembling. Making a life collage, and hoping that, if I step back far enough, if others do, an image will appear. There are a million facts, a million stories: every writer will find a different one in the same rubble. Each of us will reconceive the story. We will build an argument; we will raise a truth. It may not resemble "the truth," if there is such a thing—we may mistake someone else's opinion for fact; we may be lying or hoping for the best. Every story also pulls from the future, and in that way, it is never finished.

It will change.

If I have learned anything in Japan, about memory, about identity, it is that our narrative is what we are all looking for. A way to explain ourselves to ourselves. A way to go forward. When we look back at those moments when life changed forever, we are looking for protection against life changing again—as it does, as it is doing at this moment. It is not the witness, the writer, who creates the character, but the character who creates the witness. The function of memory is not to record history, but to tell stories. It is never fact we want.

It is understanding, fiddling with the books.

In my own story, and my image of myself, I have been waiting for my narrative to assert itself. Family, war, peace— not even chronology can bring them order: each element has to rise or fall into its place. In Japan, as a gaijin, I have lost my ability to label or declare them. I have no other eyes, or a social structure, to say what they mean and where they should go. And better still, I can continue to move them, and their buoyancy will shift. There is no balance, only the act of balancing. And therefore, there is no self. No snapshot to wave at the question: "Who am I?"

Just bits that rise and fall.

"Historically speaking, the motivation for world wars is made up and written down after the fact. When the war starts, there is a fiddling with the books. The good and bad books are kept separate.

"In the history books—it doesn't matter which one you look at—all you read about is war. When it began, when it was won, who was the hero, that sort of thing. It's a big mistake. Peace has outweighed war one hundred fold; cannons firing, guns shooting are but an instant, and yet the message of the history books is that war is a probable thing.

"If we don't record peace, how can we see that war is an aberration? There is no splendid war."

—Seventy-seven-year-old male survivor

|

# UNDERGROUND

|

THE SHADOW IS UNDERGROUND in this very modern city. Beneath the Rest House in the Peace Park, a weeping, scarred basement still echoes the blast. There is such a basement in the bank, too; where people withdrew, dying, even in the vaults where babies were born to pregnant mothers the night after the bomb. There is an Army clothing depot further from the city center whose iron shutters were bent by the blast.

When nothing else remains standing, there is still memory in the stones.

I have come to the basement of Honkawa elementary school to say goodbye to Hiroshima. The school is just across the river from the Peace Park. Only two people survived the blast here—because they were late; they were standing where I am, taking off their shoes, and the concrete sheltered them. One teacher, one student. Were they the two who spent the night in the river, as Kimiko once told the story? She is here with me, with Ami and the others. I could ask her.

The walls around us have been clawed, as if by flying glass fingernails trying to escape. Even if this is not bomb damage, it is easy to feel the past in the stale air. But it's not just the war I am feeling, it's my own past: these last seven months in Japan as I am about to leave. This visit to the basement is the last event I will attend with my friends, the Interpreters for Peace.

Next week, I will be back in New York.

There is a model in this basement, very much like the one in the Peace Museum. Hiroshima, after the bomb. I am surrounded by my friends, the people who taught me that peace is not something "between," something brokered; it can only exist within. The woman who talked of giving water to a dying man is here; the woman whose feet still burn in the summer; the man who paints the pikadon every day. And my many friends, especially Kimiko, who adopted me, saved me, and accepted me for who I am. And as we spread out around the replica of the ruined city, each person with a story and a loss, they begin to point, one by one, to the place where they were standing on that fateful morning:

*I was at the parade grounds.*

*I was in my front yard in Ushita.*

*I was on the Misasa Bridge.*

*I was in the kitchen, and my house was here.*

*I was lucky because I was in Ujina when the bomb dropped.*

And from the dimensionless cityscape, their stories return to me.

|

# KANJI

|

WHEN I CLOSE MY EYES and remember Japan, I am on the
river bank. Riding Kimiko's rusty mama-san, Olive, with its
seesawing seat and mute bell. Small wanderlust crabs scurry
across the sidewalk. Cranes graze in the shallows. Crows
call. In autumn, the sky becomes a new bruise in front of
me; in the winter, the water threads a dark ribbon through
frosty ground.

The sun and moon rise here, on the river in my mind.
They both hang—red or white or yellow—like the end of
my journey, eluding me as I ride forward as if to remind me
that this is just the prologue and the adventure is to come. I
remember once, the moon unfurled a ladder in the water so
beautiful that I stopped my bicycle at a vending machine for
a coffee and sat on the bank at midnight to watch the dance
of white amid the dance of neon, unable to decide which
was more beautiful:

*The flotilla of lanterns guide the dead safely home.*

*My fisherman, in his yellow raincoat, digs for clams.*

*The rising sun paints a pink flock of clouds.*

But it's not these images that I hold closest. It is the life:

I am breathing with my two sons beside the river. They
have been throwing themselves down that bank for so long
that my fingers are cold in my gloves and their cheeks are
bright. The point of their game is to slide on the withered

grass on the soles of their shoes—not to tumble—and they have gotten the hang of it, so the magic is now lost. I pull them over to me, and we make a pile in the poky grass, then sort ourselves to lie on our backs in three parallel lines— the symbol "kawa" for river—with our feet toward the water, our breaths puffing at the sky. I had to come all the way to Japan to find them, and if I don't know how to love them without also loving myself, I am beginning to believe they might forgive that. I have a commitment—if not an answer—to find a better way for us to be together.

This is what we have. *Ichi go, ichi e.* With every encounter, we might be changing who we are forever, and when it is over, we might never see each other again. On this early winter day, the sky is grey cotton and the river is lead, and we are being tickled by the same grass blanket at our necks. Glove to glove, holding hands: now, a different kanji.

We have hope. We are trying to read omens. When the time is right, we will know what they mean.

# OF THE DAY JUST BEGINNING
*Hiroshima, 2001*

On the river at low tide,
in the rain, there is a small sampan swinging on a pole.

The pole is twenty-five feet long and bamboo, considerably longer than the boat
or the man who leans his shoulder against it.

He is standing, in a rain jacket and hat, and a white towel tucked
under the hat to protect his neck, in a soft warm rain,
on the wide muddy river—
he is leaning on water that sighs
when the rain hits it        but otherwise doesn't move.

The boat and the man are equally still.
They are worn, and veiled by rain, clothes, tarps, and towels.

There is a black dog sitting in the bow of the boat.

Behind them, there is a bridge, weighed
down with morning traffic.
Miniature cars for the narrow street.
They are narrow, high, like single serving loaves        of Wonder bread.
They are lined up, stopped, yet revving with the energy
of the day just beginning.

They are going somewhere.  You can feel it.

The cars link the twin flanks of boxy, concrete apartment
buildings that zigzag down each river bank.
Uninspired, downright ugly,
they would be easy to condemn if you didn't know
that every single structure

had been shattered and burned in 1945.
Windows becoming scatter bombs,
beams becoming guillotines,                 beds turned into funeral pyres.
Wreckage covered in atomic ash, and then another layer.

This time, bodies.                 Flayed, ruptured, bodies that survived
for hours—powered mostly by shock and by habit
—before falling where they stood.
Women, babies.       People once.

And in the shallow river they were
heading for, the river         once so full of people desperate for a deadly drink

of water that you could walk
across their bloated bodies to avoid the fevered bridge ties,
there is now a man and a dog in a sampan.

Fishing for clams.

*With thanks to Prageeta Sharma*

# ACKNOWLEDGMENTS

I went to Hiroshima in June 2001 as a US/Japan Fellow to live for six months and to research a novel. I interviewed many survivors and spent a lot of time with the peace activists; the September 11 attacks exploded my world; my marriage unraveled. But just as memory records blame and relives joy in ways that others who were there may not agree with, this version of events is distinctly my own creation.

This narrative was written to explore how we tell our stories. The voices of the atomic bomb survivors are "fact"—culled from transcripts and translations from more thirty hibakusha testimonies. The rest I have recreated with deliberation: I have changed names, omitted extraneous details, and occasionally fiddled with the clock. Ami is a composite character—the consequence of having had so many different people help me during my time there, including more than ten interpreters. I am also sure that, over ten years, my memory has failed me. Ultimately, this memoir is best read as a reflection of who I believe myself to be as I write these words.

My deep gratitude to the US Japan Commission, the National Endowment for the Arts, and the Japanese Agency for Cultural Affairs for the fellowship that became a life-changing opportunity. The generosity and assistance of the Hiroshima community was astounding and indispensable; I could not have begun my research there without the help and friendship of so many people, including Christopher Blasdel, Professor Kan Katayanagi, Keiko Ogura, Marie Tsuruda, Masumi Takabayashi,

Hiko and Nancy Tokita, Mary Hamaji, Professor Rinjiro Sodei, Shoichi Fuji, and Kenji Mito. My wonderful guides, translators, and friends include Megumi Shimo, Mika Yoshida, Kazuko Enami, Stephen Outlaw-Spruell, Toshikazu Sumida, Noritoshi Narita, Shizuo Inoue, Michiko Yamane, and Keiko Miyamoto. I was also given great support by the Hiroshima Interpreters for Peace, the Hiroshima YMCA, the Hiroshima Peace Memorial Museum, the Chugoku Shinbun, the International House of Japan, the American Consulate in Japan, the World Friendship Center, and the Radiation Effects Research Foundation. Also, in California, the Friends of the Hibakusha. More than thirty people shared their stories with me, including Hiromu Morishita, Keiko Murakami, Michiko Yamaoka, Nobuko Ueno, Isao Aratani, Dr. Hiroe Hamano, Dixie Setoyama, Yachiyo Kato, Dr. Fumiko Kaya, Yasuko Uemoto, Suzie Sunamoto, Tatsuko Yasui, Kosuke Shishido, Pierce Fukuhara, Mitsuko Yamamoto, Nobue Hashimoto, Mamoru Hamasaki, Pe Hak Te, Chieko Tabata, Hajime Tsukamoto, Dr. and Mrs. Takeko Nakayama, Chioko Kono, Violet Kazue de Cristoforo, Tokio Yamane, Mr. Kanaoka, Akira Nakano, Katsuko Kaimatchi, Tadashi and Sumako Matsuyanagi, Yasuhiko Taketa, Dr. Kohei Daikoku, Rev. Ryoga Suwa, and the others who asked me not to acknowledge them by name. I will never forget their courage and their honesty.

I have shelves full of books on Hiroshima, the internment camps, and the Japanese Americans. Here, I want to acknowledge two indispensible works that are referenced in this text: *Where We The Enemy?: American Survivors of Hiroshima* by Rinjiro Sodei who I had the privilege of meeting at Hosei University in Tokyo (Westview Press, 1998), and *And Justice For All: An Oral History of the American Detention Camps*, by John Tateishi (Random

House, 1984). I first encountered the quote I have taken my title from in Carolyn Forche's poem "Testimony of Light" (*The Angel of History*, Harper Perennial, 1994). The poem borrows it from Peter Schwenger's book, *Letter Bomb: Nuclear Holocaust and the Exploding Word* (The Johns Hopkins University Press, 1992).

A book is more than its research, and a memoir is more than the life lived. It is born in the aftermath. To my family; to my family of friends; to my family of writer friends, and teacher friends, and student friends—to everyone who read this book in any of its many incarnations or helped bring it into the world, everyone who believed in me and lived with me while I wrestled it from life to art: thank you for your generosity, and support, and love. Although I can't name all the people who have touched it with their grace and talent during the past decade, I would like to acknowledge Kenny Fries, Beth Kephart, Eloise Flood, Bino Realuyo, Tina Nguyen, John Searcy, Prageeta Sharma, Kate Moses, Ming Yuen-Schat, Majo Tinoco, Manisha Sharma, Jonathan Hadley, Pat Klesinger, Rebecca Brown, Elena Georgiou, and Douglas A. Martin. Abiding thanks to Ellen Levine at Trident and Amy Scholder at the Feminist Press, who loved it instantly, and all the others who helped bring it into the world. And finally, my lifelong gratitude to my parents, my children, and their father who not only had to live through this, but had to live through it with a writer.